EVERYDAY ANARCHY

The Freedom of Now

STEFAN MOLYNEUX

© 2017 Stefan Molyneux
All rights reserved.

ISBN: 1975654269
ISBN 13: 9781975654269

Contents

Introduction	v
Everyday Anarchy	1
Ambivalence and Bigotry	6
Anarchy and History	8
Anarchy and Ambivalence	11
Politics and Self-Interest	12
Self-Interest and Exploitation	13
The Robber Barons	14
Anarchy and Political Leaders	19
Anarchy and the "Problem of the Commons"	22
Anarchy and Democracy	31
Anarchy and Violence	36
Anarchy and War	39
Anarchy and Protection	48
Anarchy and Morality	52
Anarchy and Education	55
Anarchy and Reform	58
Anarchy and Exceptions	61
Anarchism and Political Realities	66

The Social Challenges of Anarchism	77
Anarchism and Academia	78
Academics and Voluntarism	85
Anarchy and Socializing	90
Anarchism and Integrity	97

Introduction

It's hard to know whether a word can ever be rehabilitated – or whether the attempt should even be made.

Words are weapons, and can be used like any tools, for good or ill. We are all aware of the clichéd uses of such terms as "terrorists" versus "freedom fighters" etc. An atheist can be called an "unbeliever"; a theist can be called "superstitious." A man of conviction can be called an "extremist"; a man of moderation "cowardly." A free spirit can be called a libertine or a hedonist; a cautious introvert can be labeled a stodgy prude.

Words are also weapons of judgment – primarily moral judgment. We can say that a man can be "freed" of sin if he accepts Jesus; we can also say that he can be "freed" of irrationality if he does not. A patriot will say that a soldier "serves" his country; others may take him to task for his blind obedience. Acts considered "murderous" in peacetime are hailed as "noble" in war, and so on.

Some words can never be rehabilitated – and neither should they be. Nazi, evil, incest, abuse, rape, murder – these are all words which describe the blackest impulses of the human soul, and can never be turned to a good end. Edmund may say in King Lear, "Evil, be thou my good!" but we know that he is not speaking paradoxically; he is merely saying "that which others call evil – my self-interest – is good for me."

The word "anarchy" may be almost beyond redemption – any attempt to find goodness in it could well be utterly futile – or worse; the philosophical equivalent of the clichéd scene in hospital dramas where the surgeon blindly refuses to give up on a clearly dead patient.

Perhaps I'm engaged in just such a fool's quest in this little book. Perhaps the word "anarchy" has been so abused throughout its long history, so thrown into the pit of incontestable human iniquity that it can never be untangled from the evils that supposedly surround it.

What images spring to mind when you hear the word "anarchy"? Surely it evokes mad riots of violence and lawlessness – a post-apocalyptic Darwinian free-for-all where the strong and evil dominate the meek and reasonable. Or perhaps you view it as a mad political agenda, a thin ideological cover for murderous desires and cravings for assassinations, where wild-eyed, mustachioed men with thick hair and thicker accents roll cartoon bombs under the ornate carriages of slowly-waving monarchs. Or perhaps you view "anarchy" as more of a philosophical specter; the haunted and angry mutterings of over-caffeinated and seemingly-eternal grad students; a nihilistic surrender to all that is seductive and evil in human nature, a hurling off the cliff of self-restraint, and a savage plunge into the mad magic of the moment, without rules, without plans, without a future…

If your teenage son were to come home to you one sunny afternoon and tell you that he had become an anarchist, you would likely feel a strong urge to check his bag for black hair dye, fresh nose rings, clumpy mascara and dirty needles. His announcement would very likely cause a certain trapdoor to open under your heart, where you may fear that it might fall forever. The heavy syllables of words like "intervention," "medication," "boot camp," and "intensive therapy" would probably accompany the thudding of your quickened pulse.

All this may well be true, of course – I may be thumping the chest of a broken patient long since destined for the morgue, but certain… insights, you could say, or perhaps correlations, continue to trouble me immensely, and I cannot shake the fear that it is not anarchy that lies on the table, clinging to life – but rather, the truth.

I will take a paragraph or two to try and communicate what troubles me so much about the possible injustice of throwing the word "anarchy" into the pit of evil – if I have not convinced you by the end of the next page that something very unjust may be afoot, then I will have to continue my task of resurrection with others, because I do not for a moment imagine that I would ever convince you to call something good that is in fact evil.

And neither would I want to.

Now the actual meaning of the word "anarchy" is (from the OED):

1. Absence of government; a state of lawlessness due to the absence or inefficiency of the supreme power; political disorder.
2. A theoretical social state in which there is no governing person or body of persons, but each individual has absolute liberty (without implication of disorder).

Thus we can see that the word "anarchy" represents two central meanings: an absence of both government and social order, and an absence of government with no implication of social disorder.

Without a government…

What does that mean in practice?

Well, clearly there are two kinds of leaders in this world – those who lead by incentive, and those who lead by force. Those who lead by incentive will offer you a salary to come and work for them; those who lead by force will throw you in jail if you do not pick up a gun and fight for them.

Those who lead by incentive will try to get you to voluntarily send your children to their schools by keeping their prices reasonable, their classes stimulating, and demonstrating proven and objective success.

Those who lead by force will simply tell you that if you do not pay the property taxes to fund their schools, you will be thrown in jail.

Clearly, this is the difference between voluntarism and violence.

The word "anarchy" does not mean "no rules." It does not mean "kill others for fun." It does not mean "no organization."

It simply means: *"without a political leader."*

The difference, of course, between politics and every other area of life is that in politics, if you do not obey the government, you are thrown in jail. If you try to defend yourself against the people who come to throw you in jail, they will shoot you.

So – what does the word "anarchy" really mean?

It simply means a way of interacting with others without threatening them with violence if they do not obey.

It simply means *"without political violence."*

The difference between this word and words like "murder" and "rape" is that we do not mix murder and rape with the exact opposite actions in our life, and consider the results normal, moral and healthy. We do not strangle a man in the morning, then help a woman across the street in the afternoon, and call ourselves "good."

The true evils that we all accept – rape, assault, murder, theft – are never considered a core and necessary part of the life of a good person. An accused murderer does not get to walk free by pointing out that he spent all but five seconds of his life *not* killing someone.

With those acknowledged evils, one single transgression changes the moral character of an entire life. You would never be able to think of a friend who is convicted of rape in the same way again.

However – this is not the case with "anarchy" – it does not fit into *that* category of "evil" at all.

When we think of a society without political violence – without governments – these specters of chaos and brutality always arise for us, immediately and, it would seem, irrevocably.

However, it only takes a moment of thought to realize that *we live the vast majority of our actual lives in complete and total anarchy – and call such anarchy "morally good."*

Everyday Anarchy

For instance, take dating, marriage and family.

In any reasonably free society, these activities do not fall in the realm of political coercion. No government agency chooses who you are to marry and have children with, and punishes you with jail for disobeying their rulings. Voluntarism, incentive, mutual advantage – dare we say "advertising"? – all run the free market of love, sex and marriage.

What about your career? Did a government official call you up at the end of high school and inform you that you were to become a doctor, a lawyer, a factory worker, a waiter, an actor, a programmer – or a philosopher? Of course not. You were left free to choose the career that best matched your interests, abilities and initiative.

What about your major financial decisions? Each month, does a government agent come to your house and tell you exactly how much you should save, how much you should spend, whether you can afford that new couch or old painting? Did you have to apply to the government to buy a new car, a new house, a plasma television or a toothbrush?

No, in all the areas mentioned above – love, marriage, family, career, finances – we all make our major decisions in the complete absence of direct political coercion.

Thus – if anarchy is such an all-consuming, universal evil, why is it the default – and virtuous – freedom that we demand in order to achieve just liberty in our daily lives?

If the government told you tomorrow that it was going to choose for you where to live, how to earn your keep, and who to marry – would you fall to your knees and thank the heavens that you have been saved from such terrible *anarchy* – the *anarchy* of making your own decisions in the absence of direct political coercion?

Of course not – quite the opposite – you would be horrified, and would oppose such an encroaching dictatorship with all your might.

This is what I mean when I say that we consider anarchy to be an irreducible evil – and also an irreducible good. It is both feared and despised – and considered necessary and virtuous.

If you were told that tomorrow you would wake up and there would be no government, you would doubtless fear the specter of "anarchy."

If you were told tomorrow that you would have to apply for a government permit to have children, you would doubtless fear the specter of "dictatorship," and long for the days of "anarchy," when you could decide such things without the intervention of political coercion.

Thus we can see that we human beings are deeply, almost ferociously ambivalent about "anarchy." We desperately desire it in our personal lives, and just as desperately fear it politically.

Another way of putting this is that we love the anarchy we live, and yet fear the anarchy we imagine.

One more point, and then you can decide whether my patient is beyond hope or not.

It has been pointed out that a totalitarian dictatorship is characterized by the almost complete absence of rules. When Solzhenitsyn was arrested, he had no idea what he was really being charged with, and when he was given his 10-year sentence, there was no court of appeal, or any legal proceedings whatsoever. He had displeased someone in power, and so it was off to the gulags with him!

When we examine countries where government power is at its greatest, we see situations of extreme instability, and a marked absence of objective rules or standards. The tinpot dictatorships of third world countries are regions arbitrarily and violently ruled by gangs of sociopathic thugs.

Closer to home, for most of us, is the example of inner-city government-run schools, ringed by metal detectors, and saturated with brutality, violence, sexual harassment, and bullying. The surrounding neighborhoods are also under the tight control of the state, which runs welfare programs, public housing, the roads, the police, the buses, the hospitals, the sewers, the water, the electricity and just about everything else in sight. These sorts of neighborhoods have moved beyond democratic socialism, and actually lie closer to dictatorial communism.

Similarly, when we think of these inner cities as a whole, we can also understand that the majority of the endemic violence results from the drug trade, which directly resulted from government bans on the manufacture and sale of certain kinds of drugs. Treating drug addiction rather than arresting addicts would, it is estimated, reduce criminal activity by up to 80%.

Here, again, where there is a concentration of political power, we see violence, mayhem, shootings, stabbings, rapes and all the attendant despair and nihilism – everything that "anarchism" is endlessly accused of!

What about prisons, where political power is surely at its greatest? Prisons seethe with rapes, murders, stabbings and assaults – not to mention drug addiction. Sadistic guards beat on sadistic prisoners, to the point where the only difference at times seems to be the costumes. Here we have a "society" that seems like a parody of "anarchy" – a nihilistic and ugly universe usually described by the word "anarchy" which actually results from a maximization of political power, or the exact opposite of "anarchy."

Now, we certainly could argue that yes, it may be true that an *excess* of political power breeds anarchy – but that a *deficiency* of political power breeds anarchy as well! Perhaps "order" is a sort of Aristotelian mean, which lies somewhere between the chaos of a complete absence of political coercion, and the chaos of an excess of political coercion.

However, we utterly reject that approach in the other areas mentioned above – love, marriage, finances, career etc. We understand that *any* intrusion of political coercion into these realms would be a complete disaster for our freedoms. We do not say, with regards to marriage, "Well, we wouldn't want the government choosing *everyone's* spouse – but neither do we want the government having *no involvement* in choosing people spouses! The correct amount of government coercion lies somewhere in the middle."

No, we specifically and unequivocally reject the intrusion of political coercion into such personal aspects of our lives.

Thus once more we must at least recognize the basic paradox that we desperately need and desire the *reality* of anarchy in our personal lives – and yet desperately hate and fear the *idea* of anarchy in our political environment.

We love the anarchy we live. We fear the anarchy we imagine – the anarchy we are *taught* to fear.

Until we can discuss the realities of our ambivalence towards this kind of voluntarism, we shall remain fundamentally stuck as a species – like any individual who wallpapers over his ambivalence, we shall spend our lives in distracted and oscillating avoidance, to the detriment of our own present, and our children's future.

This is why I cannot just let this patient die. I still feel a heartbeat – and a strong one too!

Ambivalence and Bigotry

It is a truism – and I for one think a valid one – that the simple mind sees everything in black or white. Wisdom, on the other hand, involves being willing to suffer the doubts and complexities of ambivalence.

The dark-minded bigot says that all blacks are perfidious; the light-minded bigot says that all blacks are victims. The misogynist says that all women are corrupt; the feminist often says that all women are saints.

Exploring the complexities and contradictions of life with an open-minded fairness – neither with the imposition of premature judgment, nor the withholding of judgment once the evidence is in – is the mark of the scientist, the philosopher – of a rational mind.

The fundamentalists among us ascribe all mysteries to the "will of God" – which answers nothing at all, since when examined, the "will of God" turns out to be just another mystery; it is like saying that the location of my lost keys is "the place where my keys are not lost" – it adds nothing to the equation other than a teeth-gritting tautology. Mystery equals mystery. Anyone with more than half a brain can do little more than roll his eyes.

The immaturity of jumping to premature and useless conclusions is matched on the other hand only by the shallow and frightened fogs of modern – or perhaps I should say *post*-modern – relativism, where no conclusions are ever valid, no absolute statements are ever just – except that one of course – and everything is exploration, typically blindfolded, and without a compass. There is no destination, no guidepost, no sense of progress, no building to a greater goal – it is the endless dissection of cultural cadavers without even a definition of health or purpose, which thus comes perilously close to looking like fetishistic sadism.

The simple truth is that some black men are good, and some black men are bad, and most black men are a mixture, just as we all are. Some women are treacherous; some women are saints. "Blackness" or "gender" is an utterly useless metric when it comes to evaluating a person morally; it is about as helpful as trying to use an iPod to determine which way is north. The phrase "sexual penetration" does not tell us whether the act is consensual or not – saying that sexual penetration is always evil is as useless as saying that it is always good.

In the same way, some anarchism is good (notably that which we treasure so much in our personal lives) and some anarchism is bad (notably our fears of violent chaos, bomb-throwing and large mustaches). As a word, however, "anarchism" does nothing to help us evaluate these situations. Applying foolish black-and-white thinking to complex and ambiguous situations is just another species of bigotry

Claiming that "anarchism" is both rank political evil *and* the greatest treasure in our personal lives is a contradiction well worth examining, if we wish to gain some measure of mature wisdom about the essential questions of truth, virtue and the moral challenges of social organization.

Anarchy and History

Our clichéd vision of the typical anarchist tends to see him emerging shortly before World War I, which is very interesting when you think about it. The stereotypical anarchist is portrayed as a feverish failure, who uses his political ideology as a self-righteous cover for his lust for violence. He claims he wishes to free the world from tyranny, when in fact all he wants to do is to break bones and take lives.

We typically view this anarchist as a form of terrorist, which is generally defined as someone committed to the use of violence to achieve political ends, and place both in the same category as those who attempt a military *coup* against an existing government.

However, when you break it down logically, it seems almost impossible to provide a definition of terrorism which does not also include political leaders, or at least the political process itself.

The act of war is itself an attempt to achieve political ends through the use of violence – the annexation of property, the capturing of a new tax base, or the overthrow of a foreign government – and it always requires a government that is willing and able to increase the use of violence against its own citizens, through tax increases and/or the military draft. Even defending a country against invasion inevitably requires an escalation of the use of force against domestic citizens.

Thus how can we easily divide those outside the political process who use violence to achieve their goals from those *within* the political process who use violence to achieve their goals? It remains a daunting task, to say the least.

What is fascinating about the mythology of the "evil anarchists" – and mythology it is – is that even if we accept the stereotype, the disparity in body counts between the anarchists and their enemies remains staggeringly misrepresented, to say the least.

Anarchists in the period before the First World War killed perhaps a dozen or a score of people, almost all of them state heads or their representatives.

On the other hand, state heads or their representatives caused the deaths of over *10 million people* through the First World War.

If we value human life – as any reasonable and moral person must – then fearing anarchists rather than political leaders is like fearing spontaneous combustion rather than heart disease. In the category of "causing deaths," a single government leader outranks all anarchists tens of thousands of times.

Does this seem like a surprising perspective to you? Ah, well that is what happens when you look at the facts of the world rather than the stories of the victors.

Another example would be an objective examination of murder and violence in 19th-century America. The typical story about the "Wild West" is that it was a land populated by thieves, brigands and murderers, where only the "thin blue line" of the lone local sheriffs stood between the helpless townspeople and the endless predations of swarthy and unshaven villains.

If we look at the simple facts, though, and contrast the declining 19th century US murder rates with the *600,000* murders committed in the span of a few years by the government-run Civil War, we can see that the sheriffs were not particularly dedicated to protecting the helpless townspeople, but rather delivering their money, their lives and their children to the state through the brutal enforcement of taxation and military enslavement.

When we look at an institution such as slavery, we can see that it survived, fundamentally, on two central pillars – patronizing and fear-mongering mythologies, and the shifting of the costs of enforcement to others.

What justifications were put forward, for instance, for the enslavement of blacks? Well, the "white man's burden," or the need to "Christianize" and civilize these savage heathens – this was the *condescension* – and also because if the slaves were turned free, plantations would be burned to the ground, pale-throated women would be savagely violated, and all the endless torments of violence and destruction would be wreaked upon society – this was the fear-mongering mythology!

Slavery as an institution could not conceivably survive economically if the slave owners had to pay for the actual expense of slavery themselves. Shifting the costs of the capture, imprisonment and return of slaves to the general taxpayer was the only way that slavery could remain profitable. The use of the political coercion required to make slavery profitable, of course, generates a great demand for mythological "cover-ups," or ideological distractions from the violence at the core of the institution. Thus violence always requires intellectualization, which is why governments always want to fund higher education and subsidize intellectuals. We shall get to more of this later.

Even outside war, in the 20th century alone, more than 270 million people were murdered by their governments. Compared to the few dozen murders committed by anarchists, it is hard to see how the fantasy of the "evil anarchist" could possibly be sustained when we compare the tiny pile of anarchist bodies to the virtual Everest of the dead heaped by governments in one century alone.

Surely if we are concerned about violence, murder, theft and rape, we should focus on those who commit the most evils – political leaders – rather than those who oppose them, even misguidedly. If we accept that political leaders murder mankind by the hundreds of millions, then we may even be tempted to have a shred of sympathy for these "evil anarchists," just as we would for a man who shoots down a rampaging mass murderer.

ANARCHY AND AMBIVALENCE

The truth of the matter is that, as I stated above, it is clear that we have a love/hate relationship with anarchy. We yearn for it, and we fear it, in almost equal measure.

We love personal anarchy, and fear political anarchy. We desperately resist any encroachment or limitation upon our personal anarchy – and fear, mock and attack any suggestion that political anarchy could be of value.

But – how can it be possible that anarchy is both the greatest good and the greatest evil simultaneously? Surely that would make a mockery of reason, virtue and basic common sense.

Now we shall turn to a possible way of unraveling this contradiction.

Politics and Self-Interest

Truth is so often the first casualty of self-interest. In the realm of advertising, we can see this very clearly – the company that sells an anti-aging cream uses fear and insecurity to drive demand for its product. "Your beauty is measured by the elasticity of your skin, not the virtue of your soul," they say, "and no one will find you attractive if you do not look young!"

This is a rather shallow exploitation of insecurity; clearly what is *really* being sold is a definition of "beauty" that does not require the challenging task of achieving and maintaining virtue. In the short run, it is far easier, after all, to rub overpriced cream on your face than it is to start down the path of genuine wisdom and integrity.

In this way, we can see that the self-interest of the advertiser *and the consumer* are both being served in the exchange, at the expense of the truth. We all know that we shall become old and ugly – and also that this fate need not rob us of love, but rather that we can receive and give *more* love in our dotage than we did in our youth, if we live with virtue, compassion and generosity.

However, there is far less money to be made in philosophy than there is in vanity – which is another way of saying that people will pay good money to avoid the demands of virtue – and so the mutual exploitation of shallow avoidance is a cornerstone of any modern economy.

In the same way, being told that "anarchism" is just *bad, bad, bad* helps us avoid the anxiety and ambivalence we in fact feel about that which we both fear and love at the same time. Our educational and political leaders "sell" us relief from ambivalence and uncomfortable exploration – inevitably, at the expense of truth – and so far, we have been relatively eager consumers.

SELF-INTEREST AND EXPLOITATION

The CEOs of large companies receive enormous salaries for their services. Let us imagine a scenario wherein a small number of new companies grow despite having no senior managers – and appear to be making above-average profits to boot!

In this scenario, when business leadership is revealed as potentially counterproductive to profitability – or at least, unrelated to profitability – it is easy to see that the self-interest of business leaders is immediately and perhaps permanently threatened.

In addition, picture all the other groups and people whose interests would be harmed in such a scenario. Business schools would see their enrolment numbers drop precipitously; the lawyers, accountants and decorators who served these business leaders would see the demand for their services dropping; the private schools that catered to the families of the rich would be hard hit, at least for a time. Elite magazines, business shows, conventions, life coaches, haberdashers, tailors and all other sorts of other people would feel the sting of the transition, to put it mildly.

We can easily imagine that the first few companies to see increased profitability as a result of ditching their senior managers would be roundly condemned and mocked by the entrenched managers in similar companies. These companies would be accused of "cooking the books," of exploiting a mere statistical anomaly or fluke, of having secret managers, of producing shoddy goods, of "stuffing the pipe" with premature sales, of actually running at a loss, and so on.

Their imminent demise would be gleefully predicted by most if not all self-interested onlookers. The CEOs of existing companies would avoid doing business with them, and would doubtless combine a patronizing "benevolence" ("Yes, you *do* see these trends emerge once every few years – they bubble up, falter, and die out, and investors end up poorer but wiser") with fairly-open fear-mongering ("I'm not sure that it is a good career move to work at these sort of companies; I would consider it a rather black mark on the resume of any job-seeker…") and so on.

Should these new companies continue to grow, doubtless the existing business executives would get in touch with their political friends, seeking for a political "solution" on behalf of the "consumers" they wished to "protect."

Entrenched groups will always move to protect their own self-interest – this is not a bad thing, it is simply a fact of human nature. It is thus important to understand that what is called unproductive, negative, "extreme" or dangerous may indeed be so, but it is always worth looking at the motives of those who invest the time and energy to create and propagate such labels. Why are they so interested?

THE ROBBER BARONS

We can also find examples of this in the phenomenon of the "Robber Barons" in late 19th century America. The story goes that these amoral predatory monopolists were fleecing a helpless public, and so had to be restrained through the force of government anti-monopoly legislation.

If this story were really true, the first thing that we would expect is a 1-2 punch of evidence showing how prices were rising where these "monopolies" flourished – and also that it was these helpless and enraged consumers who thumped the ears of their legislators and demanded protection from the monopolists.

Of course, it would be purely absurd to imagine that this was the case, and it turns out to be a complete falsehood.

If an unjust price increase of 10%-20% was imposed upon ground beef, the net loss to the average consumer would be no more than a few pennies a week. It is incomprehensible to imagine any consumer – or group of consumers – combining their time and effort to pursue complex and lengthy legislation for the sake of opposing a tiny price increase. The cost/benefit ratio would be absurdly out of balance, since it would doubtless cost most of these consumers far more in time and money to pursue such action than they could conceivably save by reducing such an unjust price increase.

Are *you* pursuing legal action against Exxon for higher gas prices?

Of course not.

Thus to find the real culprits, we must first look at any group which can justify the pursuit of such complex and uncertain legislation; the purchasing of legislators, the writing of articles and other efforts spent to influence the media, the desperate pursuit of a highly risky venture – who could possibly justify such a mad investment?

The answer is obvious, and contains all the information we need to know to disprove the claims put forward.

The groups most harmed by these supposed-monopolists were, of course, their direct competitors. Thus we would expect that the primary – if not sole – sponsors of this legislation would not be the outraged consumers, but rather the companies competing with these "Robber Barons."

Clearly, if these monopolists were unjustly increasing prices, this would be an endless invitation for these competitors – or even outside entrepreneurs – to undercut their prices.

Ah, but perhaps these Robber Barons were achieving their monopolies through preferential political favors such as forcibly keeping competitors from entering the market.

Well, we know for certain that this could not be the case. If these Robber Barons actually did own the legislature, then their competitors would be highly unlikely to take the step of attempting to influence the legislature, because they would know it was a fight they could not win. If these "monopolists" were gaining massive and unjust profits through political favors, then their competitors who were shut out of such a lucrative system would be completely unable to funnel as much money to the legislators. Furthermore, those making the laws would be exposed to blackmail for past deals if they "switched sides" so to speak.

Thus without examining a single historical fact, we can very easily determine what actually happened, which was that:

a) The monopolists were not actually raising prices, but were lowering them, which we know because their competitors did not take the economic route of undercutting on price, but rather the political route of using the force of the state to cripple these "monopolists."
b) The monopolists were not gaining market share or unjust profits through political means, because the legislatures were still available for sale.
c) The consumers were entirely happy with the existing arrangement, which we know because the competitors had nothing to offer that the consumers would prefer to the existing state of things.

This hypothesis is amply borne out by the accurate historical evidence. Where these "Robber Barons" dominated the market, the prices of the goods they produced went down, sometimes considerably – in the case of using refrigerated railcars to store meat, a price drop of 30% was achieved in the span of a few months.

Clearly, this did not harm the interests of the consumer – but it did harm the self-interest of those attempting to compete with these highly-efficient businesses. Sadly – though, with the temptation of the government ever-present, inevitably it seems – these competitors preferred to take the political route of attacking their successful rivals through the power of the state rather than attempting to innovate themselves in turn and compete more successfully in the free market.

What about the argument that the Robber Barons used violence to create their monopolies, by threatening or killing competing workers?

Well, even if we accept this argument as true, it serves the anarchistic argument far more than the statist position.

If you hired a security guard who continually fell asleep on the job, and permitted the facility he guarded to be robbed over and over again, year after year, what would your reaction be? Would you wake him up and promote him to the rank of global manager of a highly complex security company? Would his rank incompetence at a simple task make him your ideal candidate for an enormously complex job?

Of course not.

If a government is so amoral and incompetent that it permits the murder of innocent citizens by the Robber Barons, then clearly it cannot conceivably be competent and moral enough to protect citizens from the complex economic predations of the same Robber Barons. A group that cannot perform a simple function cannot conceivably perform a far more complex function.

Over a hundred years later, we can still see how effective this propaganda really is. The specters of these "Robber Barons" still inhabit the imaginary haunted houses of our history. The role of government in controlling exploitive monopolies remains unquestioned – and how many people know the basic facts of the situation, principally that it was not the consumers who opposed these companies, but their competitors?

When we look at political "solutions" to pressing "problems," we see the same pattern over and over again. Government-run education was not instituted because parents were dissatisfied with private schools, or because children were not educated, or anything like that – but rather because the teachers wanted the job security, and cultural and religious busybodies wanted to get their hands on the tender minds of children. The "New Deal" in the 1930s was not instituted because the free market made people poor, but rather because government mismanagement of the money supply destroyed almost a quarter of the wealth of the United States.

Time and time again, we see that it is not *freedom* that leads to political control and an increase in state violence, but rather prior increases in political control and state violence.

The government does not expand its control because freedom does not work; freedom does not work because the government expands its control.

Thus we can see that freedom – or voluntarism, or anarchy – does not create problems that governments are required to "solve." Rather, propagandists lie about what the government is up to ("protecting consumers" really means "using violence to protect the profits of inefficient businesses") and the resulting expansions of political coercion and control breeds more problems, which are always ascribed to freedom.

Anarchy and Political Leaders

Clearly, there exists an entire class of people who gain immense profit, prestige and power from the existence of the government. It is equally true that, as a collective, these people have enormous control and influence over the minds of children, since it is that same government that educates virtually every child for six or more hours a day, five days a week, for almost a decade and a half of their formative years.

To analogize this situation, can we imagine that we would be at all surprised that children who came out of 14 years of religious indoctrination would in general believe in the existence and virtue of God? Would we be at all surprised if the strong arguments for atheism were left *off* a curriculum expressly designed by the priests, who directly profit from the maintenance of religious belief? In fact, we would fully expect such children to be actively trained in the rejection of arguments for atheism – inoculated against it, so to speak, so that they would react with scorn or hostility to such arguments.

We may as well hold our breath waiting for the next commercial from General Motors talking about the shortcomings of their own cars, and the virtues of their competitors' vehicles. Or perhaps we should wait for a full-color spread from McDonald's depicting detailed pictures of clogged arteries?

If so, we will wait in vain.

Similarly, when the government trains the children, how do we expect the government to portray itself? Would we expect government-paid teachers to talk openly about the root of state power, which is the initiation of the use of force against legally-disarmed citizens? Would we expect them to openly and honestly talk about the source of their income, which is the property taxes that are forcibly extracted from their students' parents?

Would we expect these same teachers to talk about how government power grows through the endless pressure and greed of special interest groups, who wish to offload the costs of the violent enforcement of their greed on the taxpayers that they in fact prey upon?

Of course not.

This is not because these teachers are evil, but rather because people respond to incentives. If the basic truths of history, logic, ethics and reality are inconvenient to those in power – as they inevitably are – those paid by those in power will almost never talk about them. We would not expect a Stalinist-era teacher to speak of the glories of capitalism; we would not expect an Antebellum teacher to teach the children of slave-owners about the evils of slavery; we would not expect an instructor at West Point to talk about the evils and corruption of the military-industrial complex, any more than we would expect the Vatican to voluntarily initiate a discussion of child abuse by Catholic priests.

We can view these basic facts without bottomless rancor, but with a gentle, almost kindly sympathy towards the inevitable trickle-down and corrupting effects of violent power.

It is no doubt a dizzying perspective to begin to examine the dark, dank and foggy jungle of propaganda with the simple light of truth, but that is what an anarchist is really all about.

An anarchist accepts the simple and basic reality that every single human being fundamentally values free choice in his or her own personal life.

An anarchist accepts the simple and basic reality that he who pays the piper always calls the tune – and that arguments against the virtue and efficacy of political power will never be disseminated in an educational system paid for by political power.

An anarchist accepts the simple and basic reality that human beings at best have an ambivalent relationship with voluntarism – and that human beings habitually avoid the discomfort of ambivalence, and so don't want to talk about anarchism any more then they want to bring up their doubts about religion during a Christian wedding ceremony.

The barriers to a reasonable understanding of the anarchistic perspective are emotionally volatile, socially isolating and almost endless. The reasonable anarchist accepts these basic facts – since facts are what anarchy is all about – and if he is truly wise, falls at least a little in love with the difficulties of his task.

We should love the difficulties we face, because if it were easy to free the world, the fact that the world is so far from being free would be completely incomprehensible…

ANARCHY AND THE "PROBLEM OF THE COMMONS"

Ask almost any professional economist what the role of government is, and he will generally reply that it is to regulate or solve the "problem of the commons," and to make up for "market failures," or the provision of public goods such as roads and water delivery that the free market cannot achieve on its own.

To anyone who works from historical evidence and even a basic smattering of first principles, this answer is, to be frank, outlandishly unfounded.

The "problem of the commons" is the idea that if farmers share common ground for grazing their sheep, that each farmer has a personal incentive for overgrazing, which will harm everyone in general. Thus the immediate self-interest of each individual leads to a collective stripping of the land.

It only takes a moment's thought to realize that the government is the *worst* possible solution for this problem – if indeed it is a problem.

The problem of the commons recognizes that where collective ownership exists, individual exploitation will inevitably result, since there is no incentive for the long-term maintenance of the productivity of whatever is collectively owned. A farmer takes good care of his own fields, because he wants to profit from their utilization in the future. In fact, ownership tends to accrue to those individuals who can make the most productive future use of an asset, since they are the ones able to bid the most when it comes up for sale. If I can make $10,000 a year more out of a patch of land than you can, then I will be willing to bid more for it, and thus will end up owning it.

Thus where there is no stake in future profitability – as in the case of publicly-owned resources – those resources inevitably tend to be pillaged and destroyed.

This is the situation that highly intelligent, well-educated people – with perfectly straight faces – say should be solved through the creation of a *government*.

Why is this such a bizarre solution?

Well, a government – and particularly the public treasury – *is the ultimate publicly-owned good*. If publicly-owned goods are *always* pillaged and exploited, then how is the creation of the largest and most violent publicly-owned good supposed to solve that problem? It's like saying that exposure to sunlight can be dangerous for a person's health, and so the solution to that problem is to throw people into the sun.

The fact that people can repeat these absurdities with perfectly straight faces is testament to the power of propaganda and self-interest.

In the same way, we are told that free-market monopolies are dangerous and exploitive. Companies that wish to voluntarily do business with us, and must appeal to our self-interest, to mutual advantage, are considered grave threats to our personal freedoms.

And – the solution that is proposed by almost everyone to the "problem" of voluntary economic interaction?

Well, since voluntary and peaceful "monopolies" are so terribly evil, the solution that is always proposed *is to create an involuntary, coercive, and violent monopoly in the form of a government.*

Thus voluntary and peaceful "monopolies" are a great evil – but the involuntary and violent monopoly of the state is the greatest good!?

Can you see why I began this book talking about our complicated and ambivalent relationship to voluntarism, or anarchy?

We see this same pattern repeating itself in the realm of education. Whenever an anarchist talks about a stateless society, he is inevitably informed that in a free society, poor children will not get educated.

Where does this opinion come from? Does it come from a steadfast dedication to reason and evidence, an adherence to well-documented facts? Do those who hold this opinion have certain evidence that, prior to public education, the children of the poor were *not* being educated? Do they genuinely believe that the children of the poor are being well-educated now? Do they seriously believe that anarchists do not care about the education of the poor? Do they believe that they are the only people who care about the education of the poor?

Of course not. This is a mere knee-jerk propagandistic reaction, like hearing a Soviet-era Red Guard boy mumbling about the necessity of the workers controlling the means of production. It is not based upon evidence, but upon prejudice.

If the "problem of the commons" and the predations of monopolies are such dire threats, then surely institutionalizing these problems and surrounding them with the endless violence of police, military and prisons would be the exact *opposite* of a rational solution!

Of course, the problem of the commons is only a problem *because* the land is collectively owned; move it to private ownership, and all is well. Thus the solution to the problem of public ownership is clearly more *private* ownership, not more *public* ownership.

Ah, say the statists, but that is just a metaphor – what about fish in the ocean, pollution in the rivers, roads in the city and the defense of the realm?

Well the simple answer to that – from an anarchist perspective at least – is that if people are not intelligent and reasonable enough to negotiate solutions to these problems in a productive and sustainable manner, then surely they are also not intelligent or reasonable enough to vote for political leaders, or participate in any government whatsoever.

Of course, there are endless historical examples of private roads and railways, private fisheries, social and economic ostracism as an effective punishment for over-use or pollution of shared resources – the endless inventiveness of our species should surely by now never fail to amaze!

The statist looks at a problem and always sees a gun as the only solution – the force of the state, the brutality of law, violence and punishment. The anarchist – the endless entrepreneur of social organization – always looks at a problem and sees an opportunity for peaceful, innovative, charitable or profitable problem-solving.

The statist looks at a population and sees an irrational and selfish horde that needs to be endlessly herded around at gunpoint – and yet looks at those who run the government as selfless, benevolent and saintly. Yet these same statists always look at this irrational and dangerous population and say: "You must have the right to choose your political leaders!"

It is truly an unsustainable and irrational set of positions.

An anarchist – like any good economist or scientist – is more than happy to look at a problem and say, "I do not know the solution" – and be perfectly happy not imposing a solution through force.

Darwin looked at the question, "Where did life come from?" and only came up with his famous answer because he was willing to admit that he did not know – but that existing religious "answers" were invalid. Theologians, on the other hand, claim to "answer" the same question with: "God made life," which as mentioned above, on closer examination, always turns out to be an exact synonym for: "I do not know." To say, "God did it," is to say that some unknowable being performed some incomprehensible action in a completely mysterious manner for some never-to-be-discovered end.

In other words: "I haven't a clue."

In the same way, when faced with challenges of social organization such as collective self-defense, roads, pollution and so on, the anarchist is perfectly content to say, "I do not know how this problem will be solved." As a corollary, however, the anarchist is *also* perfectly certain that the pseudo-answer of "the government will do it" is a total non-answer – in fact, it is an *anti*-answer, in that it provides the illusion of an answer where one does not in fact exist. To an anarchist, saying "the government will solve the problem," has as much credibility as telling a biologist – usually with grating condescension – "God created life." In both cases, the problem of infinite regression is blindly ignored – if that which exists must have been created by a God, the God which exists must have been created by another God, and so on. In the same way, if human beings are in general too irrational and selfish to work out the challenges of social organization in a productive and positive manner, then they are far too irrational and selfish to be given the monopolistic violence of state power, or vote for their leaders.

Asking an anarchist how every conceivable existing public function could be re-created in a stateless society is directly analogous to asking an economist what the economy will look like down to the last detail 50 years from now. What will be invented? How will interplanetary contracts be enforced? Exactly how will time travel affect the price of a rental car? What megahertz will computers be running at? What will operating systems be able to do? And so on and so on.

This is all a kind of elaborate game designed to, fundamentally, stall and humiliate any economist who falls for it. A certain amount of theorizing is always fun, of course, but the truth is not determined by accurate long-term predictions of the unknowable. Asking Albert Einstein in 1910 where the atomic bomb will be dropped in the future is not a credible question – and the fact that he is unable to answer it in no way invalidates the theory of relativity.

In the same way, we can imagine that abolitionists would have been asked exactly how society would look 20 years after the slaves were freed. How many of them would have jobs? What would the average number of kids per family be? Who would be working the plantations?

Though these questions may sound absurd to many people, when you propose even the vague possibility of a society without a government, you are almost inevitably maneuvered into the position of fighting a many-headed hydra of exactly such questions: "How will the roads be provided in the absence of a government?" "How will the poor be educated?" "How will a stateless society defend itself?" "How can people without a government deal with violent criminals?"

In 25 years of talking about just these subjects, I have almost never – even after credibly answering every question that comes my way – had someone sit back, sigh and say, "Gee, I guess it really *could* work!"

No, inevitably, what happens is that they come up with some situation that I cannot answer immediately, or in a way that satisfies them, and then they sit back and say in triumph, "You see? Society just *cannot* work without a government!"

What is actually quite funny about this situation is that by taking this approach, people think that they are opposing the idea of anarchy, when in fact they are completely supporting it.

One simple and basic fact of life is that no individual – or group of individuals – can ever be wise or knowledgeable enough to run society.

Our core fantasy of "government" is that in some remote and sunlit chamber, with lacquered mahogany tables, deep leather chairs and sleepless men and women, there exists a group who are so wise, so benevolent, so omniscient and so incorruptible that we should turn over to them the education of our children, the preservation of our elderly, the salvation of the poor, the provision of vital services, the healing of the sick, the defense of the realm and of property, the administration of justice, the punishment of criminals, and the regulation of virtually every aspect of a massive, infinitely complex and ever-changing social and economic system. These living man-gods have such perfect knowledge and perfect wisdom that we should hand them weapons of mass destruction, and the endless power to tax, imprison and print money – and nothing but good, plenty and virtue will result.

And then, of course, we say that the huddled and bleating masses, who could never achieve such wisdom and virtue, not even in their wildest dreams, should all get together and *vote* to surrender half their income, their children, their elderly and the future itself to these man-gods.

Of course, we never *do* get to actually see and converse with these deities. When we do actually *listen* to politicians, all we hear are pious sentiments, endless evasions, pompous speeches and all of the emotionally manipulative tricks of a bed-ridden and abusive parent.

Are these the demi-gods whose only mission is the care, nurturing and education of our precious children's minds?

Perhaps we can speak to the experts who advise them, the men behind the throne, the shadowy puppet-masters of pure wisdom and virtue? Can they come forward and reveal to us the magnificence of their knowledge? Why no, these men and women also will not speak to us, or if they do, they turn out to be even more disappointing than their political masters, who at least can make stirring if empty phrases ring out across a crowded hall.

And so, if we like, we can wander these halls of Justice, Truth and Virtue forever, opening doors and asking questions, without ever once meeting this plenary council of moral superheroes. We can shuffle in ever-growing disappointment through the messy offices of these mere mortals, and recognize in them a dusty mirror of ourselves – no more, certainly, and often far less.

Anarchy is the simple recognition that no man, woman, or group thereof is ever wise enough to come up with the best possible way to run other people's lives. Just as no one else should be able to enforce on you his choice of a marriage partner, or compel you to follow a career of his choosing, no one else should be able to enforce his preferences for social organization upon you.

Thus when the anarchist is expected to answer every possible question regarding how society will be organized in the absence of a government, any failure to perfectly answer even one of them *completely validates the anarchist's position.*

If we recognize that no individual has the capacity to run society ("dictatorship"), and we recognize that no group of elites has the capacity to run society ("aristocracy"), we are then forced to defend the moral and practical absurdity of "democracy."

Anarchy and Democracy

It may be considered a mad enough exercise to attempt to rescue the word "anarchy" – however, to smear the word "democracy" seems almost beyond folly. Fewer words have received more reverence in the modern Western world. Democracy is in its essence the idea that we all run society. We choose individuals to represent our wishes, and the majority then gets to impose its wishes upon everyone else, subject ideally to the limitations of certain basic inalienable rights.

The irrational aspect of this is very hard to see, because of the endless amount of propaganda that supports democracy (though only in democracies, which is telling), but it is impossible to ignore once it becomes evident.

Democracy is based on the idea that the majority possesses sufficient wisdom to both know how society should be run, and to stay within the bounds of basic moral rules. The voters are considered to be generally able to judge the economic, foreign policy, educational, charitable, monetary, health care, military *et al* policies proposed by politicians. These voters then wisely choose between this buffet of various policy proposals, and the majority chooses wisely enough that whatever is then enacted is in fact a wise policy – and their chosen leader then actually enacts what he or she promised in advance, and the leader's buffet of proposals is *entirely* wise, and no part of it requires moral compromise. Also, the majority is virtuous enough to respect the rights of the minority, even though they dominate them politically. Few of us would support the idea of a democracy where the majority could vote to put the minority to death, say, or steal all their property.

In addition, for even the *idea* of a democracy to work, the minority must be considered wise and virtuous enough to accept the decisions of the majority.

In short, democracy is predicated on the premises that:

A. The majority of voters are wise and virtuous enough to judge an incredibly wide variety of complex proposals by politicians.
B. The majority of voters are wise and virtuous enough to refrain from the desire to impose their will arbitrarily upon the minority, but instead will respect certain universal moral ideals.
C. The minority of voters who are overruled by the majority are wise and virtuous enough to accept being overruled, and will patiently await the next election in order to try to have their say once more, and will abide by the universal moral ideals of the society.

This, of course, is a complete contradiction. If society is so stuffed to the gills with wise, brilliant, virtuous and patient souls, who all respect universal moral ideals and are willing to put aside their own particular preferences for the sake of the common good, *what on earth do we need a government for?*

Whenever this question is raised, the shining image of the "noble citizenry" mysteriously vanishes, and all sorts of specters are raised in their place. "Well, without a government, everyone would be at each other's throats, there would be no roads, the poor would be uneducated, the old and sick would die in the streets etc. etc. etc."

This is a blatant and massive contradiction, and it is highly informative that it is nowhere part of anyone's discourse in the modern world.

Democracy is valid because just about everyone is wise and moral, we are told. When we accept this, and question the need for a government, the story suddenly reverses, and we are told that we need a government because just about everyone is amoral and selfish.

Do you see how we have an ambivalent relationship not just with anarchism, but with *democracy itself?*

In the same way, whenever an anarchist talks about a stateless society, he is immediately expected to produce evidence that every single poor person in the future will be well taken care of by voluntary charity.

Again, this involves a rank contradiction, which involves democracy.

The welfare state, old-age pensions, and "free" education for the poor are all considered in a democracy to be valid reflections of the virtuous will of the people – these government programs were offered up by politicians, and voluntarily accepted by the majority who voted for them, and also voluntarily accepted by the minority who have agreed to obey the will of the majority!

In other words, the majority of society is perfectly willing to give up an enormous chunk of its income in order to help the sick, the old and the poor – and we know this because those programs were voted for and created by democratic governments!

Ah, says the anarchist, then we already know that the majority of people will be perfectly willing to help the sick, the old and the poor in a stateless society – democracy provides empirical and incontrovertible evidence of this simple fact!

Again, when this basic argument is put forward, the myth of the noble citizenry evaporates once more!

"Oh no, without the government forcing people to be charitable, no one would lift a finger to help the poor, people are so selfish, they don't care etc. etc. etc."

This paradox cannot be unraveled this side of insanity. If a democratic government must force a selfish and unwilling populace to help the poor, then government programs do not reflect the will of the people, and democracy is a lie, and we must get rid of it – or at least stop pretending to vote.

If democracy is *not* a lie, then existing government programs accurately represent the will of the majority, and thus the poor, the sick and the old will have nothing to fear from a stateless society – and will, for many reasons, be far better taken care of by private charity than government programs.

Now it is certainly easy to just shrug off the contradictions above and it say that somewhere, somehow, there just *must be* a good answer to these objections.

Although this can be a pleasant thing to do in the short run, it is not something I have ever had much luck doing in the long term. These contradictions come back and nag at me – and I am actually very glad that they have done so, since I think that the progress of human thought utterly depends upon us taking *nothing* for granted.

The first virtue is always honesty, and we should be honest enough to admit when we do not have reasonable answers to these reasonable objections. This does not mean that we must immediately come up with new "answers," but rather just sit with the questions for a while, ponder them, look for weaknesses or contradictions in our objections – and only when we are satisfied that the objections are valid should we begin looking for rational and empirical answers to even some of the oldest and most commonly-accepted "solutions."

This process of ceasing to believe in non-answers is fundamental to science, to philosophy – and is the first step towards anarchism, or the acceptance that violence is never a valid solution to non-violent problems.

ANARCHY AND VIOLENCE

One of the truly tragic misunderstandings about anarchism is the degree to which anarchism is associated with violence.

Violence, as commonly defined, is the initiation of the use of force. (The word "initiation" is required to differentiate the category of self-defense.)

Since the word "ambivalent" seems to be the theme for this book, it is important to understand that those who advocate or support the existence of a government have themselves a highly ambivalent relationship to violence.

To understand what I mean by this, it is first essential to recognize that taxation – the foundation of any statist system – falls *entirely* under the category of "the initiation of the use of force."

Governments claim the right to tax citizens – which is, when you look at it empirically, one group of individuals claiming the moral right to initiate the use of force against other individuals.

Now, you may believe for all the reasons in the world that this is justified, moral, essential, practical and so on – but all this really means is that you have an ambivalent relationship to the use of force. On the one hand, you doubtless condemn as vile the initiation of the use of force in terms of common theft, assault, murder, rape and so on.

Indeed, it is the addition of violence that makes specific acts evil rather than neutral, or good. Sex plus violence equals rape. Property transfer plus violence equals theft. Remove violence from property transfer, and you have trade, or charity, or borrowing, or inheritance.

However, when it comes to the use of violence to transfer property from "citizens" to "government," these moral rules are not just neutralized, but actively reversed.

We view it as a moral good to resist a crime if possible – not an absolute necessity, but certainly a forgivable if not laudable action. However, to resist the forcible extraction of your property by the government is considered ignoble, and wrong.

Please note that I am not attempting to convince you of the anarchist position in this (or any other) section of this book. I consider it far too immense a task to change your mind about this in such a short work – and besides, if you are troubled by logical contradictions, I might rob you of the considerable intellectual thrill and excitement of exploring these ideas for yourself.

Thus in a democracy, we have a highly ambivalent relationship to violence itself. We both fear and hate violence when it is enacted by private citizens in pursuit of personal – and generally considered negative – goals. However, we praise violence when it is enacted by public citizens in pursuit of collective – and generally considered positive – goals.

For instance, if a poor man robs a richer man at gunpoint, we may feel a certain sympathy for the desperation of the act, but still we will pursue legal sanctions against the mugger. We recognize that relative poverty is no excuse for robbery, both due to the intrinsic immorality of theft, and also because if we allow the poor to rob the less poor, we generally feel that social breakdown would be the inevitable result. The work ethic of the poor would be diminished – as would that of the less poor, and society would in general dissolve into warring factions, to the economic and social detriment of all.

However, when we institutionalize this very same principle in the form of the welfare state, it is considered to be a noble and virtuous good to use force to take money from the more wealthy, and hand it over to the less wealthy.

Again, this book is not designed to be any sort of airtight argument against the welfare state – rather, it is designed to highlight the enormous moral contradictions in – and our fundamental ambivalence towards – the use of violence to achieve preferred ends.

ANARCHY AND WAR

I may have been doomed to this particular perspective from a very early age. I grew up in England in the 1970s, when the shadow cast by the Second World War still fell long across the mental landscape. I read war comics, saw war movies, heard details of epic battles, and sat silent during rather uncomfortable family gatherings where the British on my father's side attempted to make small talk with the Germans on my mother's.

I could not help but think, even when I was six or seven years old, that should my paternal uncle leap across the table and strangle my maternal uncle, this would be viewed as an immoral horror by everyone involved, and he would doubtless go to jail, probably for the rest of his life.

On the other hand, should they be placed in costume, and arrayed across a battlefield according to the whims of other men in costume, such a murder would be hailed as a noble sacrifice, and medals may be passed out, and pensions provided, and tickertape parades possibly ensue.

Thus, even in those long-ago days of soft white tablecloths and gently clinking cutlery, I mentally chewed on the problem that murder equals evil, and also that murder equals good. Murder equals jail, and murder equals medals.

When I was a little older, after "The Godfather" came out, endless slews of gangster movies sprayed their red gore across the silver screens. In these stories, certain tribal "virtues" such as loyalty, dedication and obeying orders, were portrayed as relatively noble, even as these butchers plied their bloody trade in slow motion, generally to the strains of classical music, and came to grimly spattered ends on bare concrete.

This paradox, too, stayed with me: "Murdering a man because another man orders you to – and pays you to – is a vile and irredeemable evil."

Then, of course, another war movie would come out, with the exact opposite moral message: "Murdering a man because another man orders you to – and pays you to – is a virtuous and courageous good."

I do remember bringing these contradictions up from time to time with the adults around me, only to be met with condescending irritation, often followed by a demand as to whether I would in fact prefer to be speaking German at present.

As I got older, and learned a little more about the world, these contradictions did not exactly resolve themselves, but rather were added to incessantly. We fought the Second World War to oppose National Socialism, I was told, as I munched on awful soy burgers, shivered in the cold and was told I could not bathe because the nationalized state unions were crippling the British economy.

I was told that I had to be terribly afraid of the selfish impulses of my fellow citizens – and also that I had to respect their wisdom when they chose a leader. I was told that the purpose of my education was to allow me to think for myself, but when I made decisions that those in authority disagreed with, I was scorned and humiliated, and my reasoning was never examined.

I was told that I should not use violence to solve my problems, but when I climbed a wall that apparently I was not supposed to, I was taken to the Headmaster's office, where he assaulted me with a cane.

I was told that the British people were the wisest, most courageous and most virtuous group on the planet – and also that I was not to disobey those in authority.

When I was taught mathematics and science, I was punished for thinking irrationally – and then, when I asked sensible questions about the existence of God, I was punished for attempting to think rationally.

I was mocked as cowardly whenever I succumbed to peer pressure – and also mocked for my lack of interest in cheering our local sports team.

When I proposed thoughts that those in authority disagreed with, they demanded that I provide evidence; when I asked that they provide evidence for *their* beliefs, I was punished for insubordination.

This is nothing peculiar to me – all children go through these sorts of mental meat grinders – but I could not help but think, as I grew up, that what passed for "thinking" in society was more or less an endless series of manipulations designed to serve those in power.

What troubled me most emotionally was not the nonsense and contradictions that surrounded me, but rather the indisputable fact that they seemed completely invisible to everyone. Well, that's not quite true. It is more accurate to say that these contradictions were visible exactly to the degree that they were avoided. Everyone walked through a minefield, claiming that it was not a minefield, but unerringly avoiding the mines nonetheless.

It became very clear to me quite quickly that I lived in a kind of negative intellectual and moral universe. The ethical questions most worth examining were those that were the most mocked, derided and attacked. What was virtuous was so often what was considered the most vile – and what was the most vile was often considered the most virtuous.

When I was 11, I went to the Ontario Science Center, which had an interesting and challenging exhibit where you attempted to trace the outline of a star by looking in a mirror. I have always remembered this exhibit, and just now I realize why – because this was my direct experience when attempting to map the ethics and virtues proclaimed by those around me – particularly those in authority.

Nowhere were these contradictions more pronounced than in the question of war.

It took me quite a long time to realize this, because the spectacle, fire and blood of war is so distracting, but the true violence of war does not occur on the battlefield, but in the homeland.

The carnage of conflict is only an *effect* of the core violence which supports war, which is the military enslavement of domestic citizens through the draft – and even more importantly, the direct theft of their money which pays for the war.

Without the money to fund a war – and pay the soldiers, whether they are drafted or not – war is impossible. The actual violence of the battlefield is a mere *effect* of the threatened violence at home. If citizens could not be forced to pay for the war – either in the present in the form of taxes, or in the future through deficit financing – then the carnage of the battlefield could never possibly occur.

I have read many books and articles on the root of war – whether it is nationalism, economic forces, faulty philosophical premises, class conflict and so on – none of which addressed the central issue, which is how war is paid for. This is like advancing merely psychological explanations as to why people play the lottery, without ever once mentioning their interest in the prize money. Why do people become doctors? Is it because they have a psychological need to present themselves as godlike healers, or because they are pleasing their mother and father, or because they are themselves secretly wounded, or because they possess an altruistic desire to heal the sick? These may be all interesting theories to pursue, but they are mere *effects* of the basic fact that doctors are highly paid for what they do.

Certainly psychological or sociological theories may explain why a particular person chooses to become a doctor rather than pursue some other high-paying occupation – but surely we should at least *start* with the fact that if doctors were *not* paid, almost no one would become a doctor. For instance, if a magic pill were invented tomorrow that ensured perfect health forever, there would be no more doctors – because no one would pay for the unnecessary service. Thus the first cause of doctors is – payment.

In the same way, we can endlessly theorize about the psychological, sociological or economic causes of war, but if we never talk about the simple fact that the first cause of war is domestic theft and military enslavement, then everything that follows remains mere abstract and airless intellectual quibbling, more designed to hide the truth than reveal it.

We can only point guns at foreign enemies because we first point guns at domestic citizens.

Without taxation, there can be no war.

Without governments, there can be no taxation.

Thus governments are the *first cause* of war.

The truth of the matter, I believe, is that deep down we know that if we pull out this one single thread – that coercion against citizens is the root of war – we know that many other threads will also come unraveled.

If we recognize the violence that is at the root of war – domestic violence, not foreign violence – then we stare at the core and ugly truth at the root of our society, and most of our collective moral aspirations.

The core and ugly truth at the root of our society is that we really, really *like* using violence to get things done. In fact, it is more than a mere aesthetic or personal preference – we define the use of violence as a moral *necessity* within our society.

How should we educate children? Why, we must force their parents – and everyone else – to pay for their education at gunpoint!

How should we help the poor? Why, we must force others in society to pay for their support at gunpoint!

How should we heal the sick? Why, we must force everyone to pay for their medical care at gunpoint!

Now, it may be the case that we have exhausted all other possibilities and ways of dealing with these complex and challenging problems, and that we have been forced to fall back on coercion, punishment and control as regretful necessities, and we are constantly looking for ways to reduce the use of violence in our solutions for these problems.

However, that is not the case, either empirically or rationally.

The education of poor children, the succor of the impoverished and the healing of the sick all occurred through private charities and voluntary associations long before statist agencies displaced them. This is exactly what you would expect, given the general modern support for these state programs, because everyone is so concerned with these genuinely needy groups.

Where violence is considered to be a regrettable but necessary solution to a problem, those in authority do not shy away from talking openly about it. When I was a child in England in the 1970s, I was repeatedly told with pride by my elders about their courageous use of violence against the Axis powers in World War II. No one tried to give me the impression that the Nazis were defeated by cunning negotiation and psychological tricks. The endless slaughterhouses of both the First and Second World Wars were not kept hidden from me, but rather the violence was praised as a regrettable but moral necessity.

American children are told about the nuclear attacks on Nagasaki and Hiroshima – the slaughter and radiation poisoning of hundreds of thousands of Japanese civilians is not kept a secret; it is not bypassed, ignored or repressed in the telling of the tale.

Even when the war in question was itself questionable, such as the war in Vietnam, no one shies away from the true nature of the conflict, which was endless genocidal murder.

I do not for a moment believe that all of these genocides and slaughters were morally justifiable – or even practically required – but mine is certainly a minority opinion, and since the majority believes that these murders were both morally justified and practically required, they feel fully comfortable openly discussing the violence that they consider unavoidable.

However, this is not the case when we talk about statist solutions to the problems of charity and ill health. You could spend an entire academic career in these fields, and read endless books and articles on the subject, and never once come across any reference to the fact that these solutions are funded through violence. Just so you can understand how strange this really is, imagine spending 40 years as a professional war historian, and never once coming across the idea that war involves violence. Would we not consider that a rather egregious evasion of a rather basic fact?

This is a rather volatile comparison I know, but we saw the same phenomenon occurring in Soviet Russia. Almost no reference was made to the gulags in official state literature, particularly that literature intended to be consumed overseas. The tens of millions of concentration camp inmates showed up nowhere in the general or academic narrative of the Soviet Union – when the book "One Day in the Life of Ivan Denisovich" finally appeared, even this relatively mild account of a day in the life of a prison camp inmate was greeted with shock, derision, horror and rage by those charged with defending that narrative.

It cannot really be the case that when society is genuinely proud of something, the truth is kept mysteriously hidden from view. Can we imagine fans of the New York Yankees actively working to repress the fact that their team won the World Series? Can we imagine the Communist leaders of China suppressing news that their athletes had won gold medals in the Olympics? Can we imagine a police department feverishly working to censor the facts about a large reduction in the crime rate?

Of course not. Where we are genuinely proud of an achievement, we do not refrain from talking about its causes. An Olympic athlete will speak with pride about the years of endless dawn training sessions; a successful entrepreneur will not hide the decades of hard work it took to succeed; a woman who has successfully struggled to lose weight is unlikely to wear a fat suit when she goes to her high school reunion.

However, when a core reality conflicts with a mythological narrative, academics, intellectuals and other cultural leaders are well-compensated for their ability to completely ignore that core reality – and usually savagely attack and mock anyone who brings it up.

ANARCHY AND PROTECTION

One core reality that anarchists focus on – which surely is at least worthy of discussion – is that governments claim to serve and protect their citizens. When I was a child, and questioned the ethics of World War II, I was asked if I would prefer to be speaking German. In other words, the brave men and women of the Allied forces spent their lives and blood defending me from foreign marauders who would have enslaved me. This approach reinforces the basic story that the government was trying to protect its citizens.

In the same way, when I question the use of violence in the supplying of education, people always tell me that in the absence of that violence – even if they admit to its existence – the poor would remain uneducated. This approach reinforces the basic story that the purpose of state violence in this realm is to educate the children.

You can see the same pattern just about everywhere else. When I talk about the violence of the war on drugs, I am told that without such a war, society would degenerate into nihilistic addiction and violence – thus the purpose of the war on drugs is to keep people off drugs, and their neighbours safe from violence. When I talk about the base and coercive predation of Social Security, I am told that without it, the old would starve in the streets – thus reinforcing the narrative that the purpose of Social Security is to provide an income for the old, without which they would starve.

When we examine the narrative that the state exists to protect its citizens, we can clearly see that if we unearth the basic reality of the violence of taxation, a malevolent contradiction emerges.

It is very hard for me to tell you that I am only interested in protecting you, if I attack you first. If I roll up to you in a black van, jam a hood over your head, throw you in the back of my van, tie you up and toss you in my basement, would you reasonably accept as my explanation for this savagery that I only wished to keep you from harm?

Surely you would reply that if I was really interested in keeping you from harm, why on earth would I kidnap you and lock you up in a little room? Surely, if I initiate the use of force against you, it is somewhat irrational (to say the least) for me to tell you that I am only acting to protect you from the use of force.

This is a central reason why the aggression that governments initiate against their own citizens in order to extract the cash and cannon fodder for war is never talked about. It is hard to sustain the thesis that governments exist to protect their citizens if the first threat to citizens is always their own government.

If I have to rob you in order to pay for "protecting" your property from theft, at the very least I have created an insurmountable logical contradiction, if not a highly ambivalent moral situation.

In general, where coercion is a regrettable but necessary means of achieving a moral good, that coercion is not hidden from general view. In police dramas, the violence of the cops is not hidden. In war movies, shells, bullets and limbs fly across the screen with wanton abandon.

However, the coercion at the root of war and state social programs remains forever unspoken, unacknowledged, repressed, hidden from view; it is mad, shameful and imprudent to speak of it.

A hunter who proudly displays a dead deer on the hood of his car, and puts the antlers up in his basement, and barbecues the venison for his friends, can be considered somewhat proud – or at least not ashamed – of his hobby.

A hunter who uses a silencer, shoots a deer in the middle of the night, and carefully buries the body, leaving no trace, cannot be considered at all proud – and is in fact utterly ashamed – of his hobby.

Thus, when an anarchist looks at society, he sees a desperate shame regarding the use of violence to achieve social ends such as the military, health care, and education. Any anarchist who has even a passing interest in psychology – and I certainly put myself in this category – understands that this kind of unspoken shame is utterly toxic, both to an individual and to a society.

Thus it inevitably falls to anarchists to perform the unpleasant task of digging up the "body in the backyard," or pointing out the widespread, prevalent and ever-increasing use of violence to achieve moral goals within society. "Is this right?" asks the anarchist – fully aware of the hostile and resentful glances he receives from those around him. "How can violence be both the greatest evil and the greatest good?" "If the violence that we use to achieve our supposedly moral ends is in fact justified and good, why is it that we are so ashamed to speak of it?"

To be an anarchist, to say the very least, requires a strong hide when it comes to social hostility and disapproval.

When people have genuinely exhausted all other possibilities, they tend not to be ashamed of their eventual solution. Even if we take the surface narrative of the Second World War at face value, the victors were able to express just pride because the narrative included the significant caveat that there was no other possible response to the aggression of the German, Italian and Japanese fascists.

Parents tend to be pretty open about hitting their children if they genuinely believe that no rational or moral alternatives exist to the use of violence. If hitting a child is the only way to teach her to be a good, productive and rational adult, then *not* hitting her is obviously a form of lax parenting, if not outright abuse. Hitting your daughter thus becomes a form of moral responsibility, and thus a positive good, much like yanking her back from running into traffic and ensuring that she eats her vegetables.

Such a parent, of course, reacts with outrage and indignation if you suggest to him that there are more productive alternatives to violence when it comes to raising children – for the obvious reason that if those alternatives exist, his violence turns from a positive good to a moral evil.

This is the situation that an anarchist faces when he talks about nonviolent alternatives to existing coercive "solutions." If there is a nonviolent way to help the poor, heal the sick, educate the children, protect property, build roads, defend a geographical area, mediate disputes, punish criminals and so on – then the state turns from a regretfully necessary institution to an outright criminal monopoly.

This is a rather large and jagged pill for people to swallow, for any number of psychological, personal, professional and philosophical reasons.

ANARCHY AND MORALITY

Another paradox that anarchy brings into uncomfortable view is the contradiction between coercion and morality.

We all in general recognize and accept the principle that where there is no choice, there can be no morality. If a man is told to commit some evil while he has a gun pressed to his head, we would have a hard time categorizing him as evil – particularly compared to the man who is pressing the gun to his head.

If we accept the Aristotelian view that the purpose of life is happiness, and we accept the Socratic view that virtue brings happiness, then when we deny choice to people, we deny them the capacity for virtue, and thus for happiness.

There is great pleasure in helping others – I would certainly argue that it is one of the greatest pleasures, outside of love itself, which encompasses it. Helping others, though, is a highly complex business, which requires detailed personal attention, rigorous standards, a combination of encouragement, sternness, enthusiasm, sympathy and discipline – to name just a few!

Using coercion to drive charity is like using kidnapping to create love. Not only does the use of coercion through state programs deny choice to those wishing to help the poor – and thus the joy of achievement, and the motivation of happiness – but it corrupts and destroys the complex interchange required to elevate a human soul from its meager surroundings and its own low expectations.

If we believe that violence is a valid way to achieve moral ends – of helping the poor for instance – then there are two other approaches which would be far more logically consistent than the forced theft and transfer of taxation.

If violence is the only valid way to create economic "equality," then surely it would make far more sense to simply allow those below a certain level of income to steal the difference from others. If we understand that state welfare agencies skim an enormous amount of money off the top – they represent a truly savage expense – then we can easily eliminate this overhead, and have a far more rational system besides, simply by eliminating the middleman and allowing the poor to steal from the middle and upper classes.

If the prospect of this solution fills you with horror, that is important to understand. If you feel that this proposal would degenerate into armed gangs of the poor rampaging through wealthier neighborhoods, then you are really saying that the poor are poor because they lack restraint and judgment, and will pillage others and undermine the economic success and general security of society in order to satisfy their own immediate appetites, without thought for the future.

If this is the case – if the poor really are such a shortsighted and savage band – then it is clear that they do not have the judgment and self-control to vote in democratic elections – which are essentially about the forcible transfer of income. If the poor only care about satisfying their immediate appetites, without a care for the long term, then they should not be at all involved in the coercive redistribution of wealth in society as a whole.

Ah, but what if taking the right to vote away from the poor fills you with outrage? Very well, then we can assume that the poor are rational, and able and willing to defer gratification. If a man is wise enough to vote on the use of force, then he is certainly wise enough to use that force himself.

Indeed, the barriers to using force *personally* are far higher than voting for the use of force in a democratic system. If you have to pick up a gun and go and collect your just property from richer people, that is quite a high "barrier to entry." If, on the other hand, you simply have to scribble on the ballot once every few years, and then sit back and wait for your check to arrive, surely that will drive the escalation of violence in society far more rapidly.

If you still feel that this solution would be disastrous, because the poor would act with bad judgment, then you face a related issue, which is the quality of the education that the poor have received.

ANARCHY AND EDUCATION

If the poor lack wisdom, knowledge and good judgment, but they have been educated by the government for almost 15 years straight, then surely if we believe that the poor can be educated, we must then blame the government for failing to educate them. Since the poor cannot afford private schools, they must surrender their children to government schools, which have a complete and coercive monopoly over their education.

Now, either the poor have the capacity for wisdom and efficacy, or they do not. If the poor *do* have the capacity for wisdom, then the government is fully culpable for failing to cultivate it through education. If the poor do not have the capacity for wisdom, then the government is fully culpable for wasting massive resources in a futile attempt to educate them – and also, they cannot justly be allowed to vote.

Again, although I know that this must be uncomfortable or annoying to read through, I am willing myself to refrain from providing the clear and moral anarchistic solutions to these seemingly intractable problems. There is no point trying to give society a pill if society does not even think that it is sick. If your appendix is inflamed, and I offer to remove it for you, you will doubtless cry out your gratitude – if I run up to you on the street, however, and offer to remove an appendage that you believe to be both necessary and healthy, you would be highly inclined to charge me with assault.

Given that anarchism represents a near complete break with political society – although, as described above, a highly moral and rational expansion of personal society – it remains in no way attractive if nothing is seen to be particularly wrong with political society.

Churchill once famously remarked: "Democracy is the worst form of government, except for all those other forms that have been tried from time to time." Anarchists believe this to be true, but would add that no form of government is better than no government at all!

This is not to say that democracy is not a better form of government than tyranny. It certainly is – my problem is that we have in the West achieved democracy over the past few hundred years, and now seem to be eternally content to rest on our laurels, so to speak.

I spent almost 15 years as a software entrepreneur, which may have colored my perspective on this issue to some degree. The software field reinvents itself almost from the ground up every year or two, it seems, which demands a constant commitment to dynamism, continual learning, and the abandonment of prior conceptions. The swift currents of perpetual change quickly sweep the inert away.

Thus I fully appreciate the significant step forward represented by democracy – but the mere fact that a thing is "better" in no way indicates that it is "best."

When medieval surgeons realized that a patient had a better chance of surviving gangrene if they hacked off a limb, this could surely be called a better solution – but it could scarcely be called the best *possible* solution. Recognizing that prevention is always better than a cure does not mean that all cures are equally good.

I have no doubt whatsoever that the first caveman to figure out how to start a fire shared his knowledge with his tribe, and they all sat in a cave, with their feet pointed towards the flickering flames, warm in the midst of a winter chill for the first time, and grunted at each other: "Well, it can't *possibly* get any better than this!"

No doubt when, a thousand years later, someone figured out that it was easier to capture and domesticate a cow rather than to continually hunt game, everyone sat back in front of their fire, their bellies full of milk, and grunted at each other: "Well, it can't *possibly* get any better than this!"

These things are genuine improvements, to be sure, and we should not ever fail to appreciate the progress that we make – but neither should we automatically and endlessly assume that every step forward is the final and most perfect step, and that nothing can ever conceivably be improved in the future.

Democracy is considered to be superior to tyranny – and rightly so I believe – because to some degree it imitates the feedback mechanisms of the free market. Politicians, it is said, must provide goods and services to citizens, who provide feedback through voting.

It would seem to be logical to continue to extend that which makes democracy work further and further. If I find that, as a doctor, I infect fewer of my patients when I wash one little finger, then surely it would make sense to start washing other parts of my hand as well.

Really, this is what my approach to anarchism is fundamentally about. If voluntarism and feedback – a quasi-"market" – is what makes democracy superior, then surely we should work as hard as possible to extend voluntarism and feedback – particularly since we have the example of real markets, which work spectacularly well.

Anarchy and Reform

There is a great fear among people – or a great desire, to be more accurate – with regards to abandoning this system, when the perception exists that it can be reformed instead.

Democracy is messy, it is said – politicians pander to special interests, court voters with "free" goodies, manipulate the currency to avoid directly increasing taxes, create endless and intractable problems in the realms of education, welfare, incarceration and so on – but let's not throw the baby out with the bathwater! If you have good ideas for improving the system, you should get involved, not sit back in your armchair and criticize everything in sight! One of the rare privileges of a living in a democracy is that anyone can get involved in the political process, from running for a local school board to prime minister or president of the entire country! Letter-writing campaigns, grassroots activism, blogs, associations, clubs – you name it, there are countless ways to get involved in the political process.

Given the degree of feedback available to the average citizen of a democracy, it makes little sense to agitate for changing the system as a whole. Since the system is so flexible and responsive, it is impossible to imagine that it can be replaced with any system that is more flexible – thus the practical ideal for anyone interested in social change is to bring his ideas to the "marketplace" of democracy, see who he can get on board, and implement his vision within the system – peacefully, politically, *democratically*.

This is a truly wonderful fairy tale, which has only the slight disadvantage of having nothing to do with democracy whatsoever.

When we think of a truly free market – otherwise known as the "free market" – we understand that we do not have to work for years and years, and give up thousands of hours and tens or hundreds of thousands of dollars, to satisfy our wishes. If I want to shop for vegetarian food, say, I do not have to spend years lobbying the local supermarket, or joining some sort of somewhat ineffective advisory Board, and pounding lawn signs, and writing letters, and cajoling everyone in the neighborhood – all I have to do is go and buy some vegetarian food, locally or over the Internet if I prefer.

If I want to date a particular woman, I do not have to lobby everyone in a 10 block radius, get them to sign a petition, make stirring speeches about my worthiness as a boyfriend, devote years of my life attempting to get collective approval for asking her out. All I have to do is walk up to her, ask her out and see if she says "yes."

If I want to be a doctor, I do not have to spend years lobbying every doctor in the country to get a majority approval for my application. Neither do I have to pursue this process when I want to move, drive a car, buy a book, plan for my retirement, change countries, learn a language, buy a computer, choose to have a child, go on a diet, start an exercise program, go into therapy, give to a charity and so on.

Thus it is clear that individuals are "allowed" to make major and essential life decisions without consulting the majority. The vast majority of our lives is explicitly anti-democratic, insofar as we vehemently reserve the right to make our own decisions – and our own mistakes – without subjecting them to the scrutiny and authority of others. Why is it that we are "allowed" to choose who to marry, whether to have children, and how to raise them – but we are violently *not* allowed to openly choose where they go to school? Why is every decision that leads up to the decision of how to educate a child is completely free, personal, and anti-democratic – but the moment that the child needs an education, a completely *opposite* methodology is enforced upon the family? Why is the free anarchy of personal decisions – in direct opposition to coercive authority – such a moral imperative for every decision which leads *up* to the need for a child's education – but then, free anarchic choice becomes the greatest imaginable evil, and coercive authority must be substituted in its place?

There is a particularly cynical side of me – which is not to say that the cynicism is necessarily misplaced – which would argue that the reason that there is no direct interference in having children is because that way people will have more kids, which the state needs to grow into taxpayers, in the same way that a dairy farmer needs his cows to breed. Those who profit from political power always need new taxpayers, but they certainly do not want independently critical and rational taxpayers, since that is fundamentally the opposite of being a taxpayer. Thus they do not interfere with *having* children, only with the *education* of children – just as a goose farmer will not interfere with egg laying, but will certainly clip the wings of any geese he wishes to keep alive and profit from.

Anarchy and Exceptions

At this point, you may be thinking that there are good reasons why political coercion is substituted for personal anarchy in particular situations. Perhaps there is some rule of thumb or principle which separates the two which, if it can be discovered, will lay this mystery bare.

If I break up with a girlfriend, for instance, I do not owe her anything legally. If I marry her, however, I do. When I take a new job, I may be subject to a probationary period of a few months, when I can be fired – or quit – with impunity. We can think of many examples of such situations – the major difference, however, is that these are all voluntary and contractual situations.

The justification for a government – particularly a democratic government – is really founded upon the idea of a "social contract." Because we happen to be born in a particular geographical location, we "owe" the government our allegiance, time, energy and money for the rest of our lives, or as long as we stay. This "contract" is open to renegotiation, insofar as we can decide to alter the government by getting involved in the political process – or, we can leave the country, just as we can leave a marriage or place of employment. This argument – which goes back to Socrates – is based upon an implied contract that remains in force as long as we ourselves remain within the geographical area ruled over by the government.

However, this idea of the "social contract" fails such an elemental test that it is only testament to the power of propaganda that it has lasted as a credible narrative for over 2,000 years.

Children cannot enter into contracts – and adults cannot have contracts imposed upon them against their will. Thus being born in a particular location does not create any contract, since it takes a lunatic or a Catholic to believe that obligations accrue to a newborn squalling baby.

Thus children cannot be subjected to – or be responsible for – any form of implicit social contract.

Adults, on the other hand, must be able to choose which contracts they enter into – if they cannot, there is no differentiation between imposing a contract on a child, and imposing a contract on an adult. I cannot say that implicit contracts are invalid for children, but then they magically become automatically valid when the child turns 18, and bind the adult thereby.

It is important also to remember that there is fundamentally no such thing as "the state." When you write a check to pay your taxes, it is made out to an abstract quasi-corporate entity, but it is cashed and spent by real life human beings. Thus the reality of the social contract is that it "rotates" between and among newly elected political leaders, as well as permanent civil servants, appointed judges, and the odd consultant or two. This coalescing kaleidoscope of people who cash your check and spend your money is really who you have your social contract with. (This can occur in the free market as well, of course – when you take out a loan to buy a house, your contract is with the bank, not your loan officer, and does not follow him when he changes jobs.)

However, to say that the same man can be bound by a unilaterally-imposed contract represented by an ever-shifting coalition of individuals, in a system that was set up hundreds of years before he was born, without his prior choice – since he did not choose where he was born – or explicit current approval, is a perfectly ludicrous statement.

We can generally accept as unjust any standard of justice that would disqualify itself. When we are shopping, we would scarcely call it a "sale" if prices had been jacked up 30%. We would not clip a "coupon" that added a dollar to the price of whatever we were buying – in fact, we would not call this a coupon at all!

If we examine the concept of the "social contract," which is claimed as a core justification for the existence of a government, it is more than reasonable to ask whether the social contract would justly enforce the social contract itself! In other words, if the government is morally justified because of the ethical validity of an implicit and unilaterally imposed contract, will the government defend implicit and unilaterally imposed contracts? If I start up a car dealership and automatically "sell" a car to everyone in a 10 block radius, and then send them a bill for the car they have "bought" – and send them the car as well, and bind their children for eternity in such a deal as well – would the government enforce such a "contract"?

I think that we all know the answer to that question…

If I attempted to bring a social contract to an agency that claims as its justification the existence and validity of the exact same social contract, it would laugh in my face and call me insane.

Are you beginning to get a clear idea of the kind of moral and logical contradictions that a statist system is based upon?

Many times throughout human history, certain societies have come to the valid conclusion that an institution can no longer be reformed, but must instead be abolished. The most notable example is slavery, but we can think of others as well, such as the unity of church and state, oligarchical aristocracy, military dictatorships, human or animal sacrifices to the gods, rape as a valid spoil of war, torture, pedophilia, wife abuse and so on. This does not mean of course that all of these practices and institutions have faded from the world, but it does mean that in many civilized societies, the essential debate is over, and was not settled with the idea of "reforming" institutions such as slavery. The origin of the phrase "rule of thumb" came from an attempt to reform the beating of wives, and restrict it to beating your wife with a stick no wider than your thumb. This practice was not reformed, but rather abolished.

However well-intentioned these reforms may have been, we can at best only call them ethical in terms of halting steps towards the final goal, which is the elimination of the concept of wife beating as a moral norm at all. In the same way, some reformers attempted to get slave owners to beat their slaves less, or at least less severely, but with the hindsight of history and our further moral development, we can see that slavery was not fundamentally an institution that could ever be reformed, but rather had to be utterly abolished. We can find encouragement in such "reforms" only to the degree that they reduced suffering in the present, while hopefully spurring on the goal of abolishing slavery.

Any moralist who said that getting rid of slavery would be a criminal and moral disaster of the first order, but instead encouraged slaves to attempt to work within the system, or counseled slave owners to voluntarily take on the goal of treating their slaves with less brutality, could scarcely be called a moralist, at least by modern standards. Instead, we would term such a "reformer" as a very handy apologist for the existing brutality of the system. By pretending that the evils inherent in slavery could be mitigated or eliminated through voluntary internal reform, these "moralists" actually slowed or stalled the progress towards abolition in many areas. By holding out the false hope that an evil institution could be turned to goodness, these sophists blunted the power of the argument from morality, which is that slavery is an inherent evil, and thus cannot be reformed.

The finger-wagging admonition, "Rape more gently," is oxymoronic. Rape is the opposite of gentle, the opposite of moral.

This is how many anarchists view the proposition that the existing system of political violence should be reformed somehow from within, rather than fundamentally opposed on moral terms, as an absolute evil, based on coercion and brutality, particularly towards children – with the inevitable consequence that its only salvation can come from being utterly abolished.

Anarchism and Political Realities

Along with the anarchistic moral arguments against the use of force to solve problems come many well-developed economic arguments against the long-term stability of any democratic political system.

To take just one example, let's look at the problem of unequal incentives.

In the United States, thousands of sugar producers receive massive state subsidies and coercive protection from foreign competitors – benefits which have been in place, for the most part, since the close of the war of 1812. Although $1.2 billion was spent in 2005 subsidizing sugar production, the majority of the money goes to a few dozen growers.

These sugar subsidies cost the US economy billions of dollars annually, while netting major sugar producers millions of dollars a year each. The average American consumer would have to fight for years, spend untold hours and dollars attempting to overturn the subsidies in Congress – to save, what? A few dollars a year apiece? None but a lunatic would attempt it.

On the other hand, of course, these sugar growers will spend whatever time and money it takes to preserve their massive influx of cash. It is not that hard to figure out who will present stronger "incentives" – to say the least – to Congress. It is not that hard to figure out just who will donate as much as humanly possible to a Congressman's run. It is embarrassingly easy to figure out who will keep calling the congressman at 2 a.m. with dire threats should he dare to question the value of the subsidies, and promises of money if he refrains.

Politicians, like so many of us, take the rational path of least resistance. A congressman will receive no thanks for killing these subsidies and returning a few unproven and ignored dollars to his average constituent's pocket – such a "benefit" would scarcely even be noticed. However, the sugar growers would raise bloody hell to the very skies, as would all their employees, their hangers on, the professionals they employ, and anyone else who benefits from the concentration of illicit wealth that they enjoy.

Furthermore, should the subsidies be somehow cut, and the price of a candy bar dropped a nickel, all that would happen is that some *other* politician would impose a tax of, say, about a nickel on candy bars – to save the children's *teeth*, of course – thus generating more cash for *him* to hand out and utterly nullifying any benefit to the consumer. Would any rational politician pursue a policy that would enrage his supporters, strengthen his enemies and win no new friends?

Of *course* not.

Thus it is clear to see that while no incentive exists to do the right thing, every conceivable incentive exists to do the wrong thing. In the case of sugar subsidies, the "sting" to the consumer is only a few dollars a year – multiply this, however, thousands and thousands of times over, for each special interest group, and we can see how the taxpayer will inevitably die a death not by beheading, but rather by the tiny bites of 10,000 mosquitoes, each feeding its young by feasting on a droplet of his blood.

No democratic government has ever survived without taking a monopoly control over the currency. The reason for this is simple – politicians need to buy votes, but that illusion is hard to sustain if those you give money to have to pay that money back within a few years in the form of higher taxes. Taxpayers would get wise to this sort of game very quickly, and so politicians need to find other ways to fog and befuddle taxpayers. Deficit financing is one way – give money to people in the present, then stick the bill to their children at some undefined point in the future, when you're no longer around – perfect!

Another great way of pretending to give people money is to inflate their currency by printing more money. This way, you can give a man a hundred dollars today, and just reduce the purchasing power of his dollar by 5% next year by printing more. Not one person in a thousand will have any idea what's really going on, and besides, you always have the business community to blame for "gouging" the consumer.

Another "solution" is to promise public-sector unions large increases in salary, which only really take effect toward the end of your office, so that the next administration gets stuck with the real bill. Also, you can sign perpetual contracts giving them plenty of medical and retirement benefits, the majority of which will only kick in when they get older, long after you are gone.

Alternatively, you can sell long-term bonds that give you the cash right now, while sticking future taxpayers in 10, 20 or 30 years with the bill for repaying your principle, and accumulated interest.

One other option is to start licensing everything in sight – building permits, hot dog stand permits, dog licenses and so on – thus grabbing a lot of cash up front, and leaving your successors to deal with the diminished tax base from lower economic activity in the future.

Or you can buy the votes of apartment-dwellers with "rent control" – leaving the next few administrations to deal with the inevitable resulting apartment shortage.

This list can go on and on – it is a list as old as the Roman and Greek democracies – but the essential point is that democracy is always and forever utterly unsustainable.

A basic fact of economics is that people respond to incentives – the incentives in any statist society – democratic, fascist, communist, socialist, you name it – are always so unbalanced as to turn the public treasury into a kind of blood mad shark-driven feeding frenzy.

Well, say the defenders of democracy, but the people can always choose to vote in other people who will fix the system!

One of the wonderful aspects of working from first principles, and taking our evidence from the real world, is that we don't have to believe pious nonsense anymore. Except directly after significant wars, when they need to re-grow their decimated tax bases, democratic governments simply never *ever* get smaller.

The logic of this remains depressingly simple, and just as depressingly inevitable.

A central question that any voter who claims to wish to be informed must ask is: *why is this man's name on the ballot?*

The standard answer is that he has a vision to fix the neighborhood, the city, or the country, and so he has nobly dedicated his life to public service, and needs your vote so that he can begin fixing the problem. He is a pragmatic idealist who knows that compromises must be made, but who can still make tangible improvements in your life.

Of course, this is all pure nonsense, as we can well see from the fact that things in a democracy always get worse, not better. Standards of living decline, national debt explodes, household debt increases, educational achivements plummet, poverty rates increase, incarceration rates increase, unfunded liabilities skyrocket – and yet, election after election, the sheep run to the polls and feverishly scribble their hopes on to the ballots, certain that *this* time, everything will turn around! (For those reading this in the future, we are currently right in the middle of "Obama-mania.")

The question remains – *why is this man on the ballot?*

We all know that it takes an enormous amount of money and influence to run for any kind of substantial office. The central question is, then: *why do people give money to a candidate?*

I'm not talking about a national presidential campaign, where obviously people give a lot of money to the candidate in the hopes of giving him power to achieve some sort of shared goals and so on.

No, I mean: where does the money to get *started* even come from?

Why would pharmaceutical companies, aerospace companies, engineering companies, manufacturing companies, farmers, and public-sector unions and so on give money and support to a candidate?

Clearly, these groups are not handing out cash for purely idealistic reasons, since they are in the business of making money, at least for their members. Thus they must be giving money to potential candidates in return for political favors down the road – preferential treatment, tax breaks, tariff restrictions on competitors, government contracts etc.

In other words, any candidate that *you* get to vote for must have already been bought and paid for by others.

Does this sound like an odd and cynical assertion? Perhaps – but it is very easy to figure out if a candidate has been bought and paid for.

Candidates will always talk in stirring tones about "sacrifice" and so on, but you surely must have noticed by now that no candidate ever talks *specifically* about the spending that he is going to cut. You never hear him say that he is going to balance the budget by cutting the spending of X, Y or Z. Everything is either couched in abstract terms, or specific promises to specific groups. (At the moment, the current fetish – in leftist circles – is to pretend that 47 million Americans can get "free" healthcare if the government lowers the tax breaks on a few billionaires.)

In other words, if you don't see anyone else's head on the chopping block, that is because it is *your* head on the chopping block.

Of course, if the government *really* wanted to help the economy at the expense of some very rich people, it would simply annul the national debt – in effect, declare bankruptcy, and start all over again.

Why does it not do this? Why does it never even *approach* this topic? We have seen price controls on a variety of goods and services over the past few generations – why not simply place a moratorium on paying interest on the national debt, at least for the time being?

Well, the simple answer is that the government simply cannot survive without a constant infusion of loans, largely from foreign lenders.

This is a bit of a clue for you as to how important your vote really is, and how concerned your leaders are about your personal and particular issues – relative to, say, those of foreign lenders.

Ah, you might argue, but why would a pharmaceutical company, say, give money to a potential candidate, since no deal can possibly be put down in writing, and that potential candidate might well take the money, and then just not take the calls from that pharmaceutical company when he or she gets into power?

Well, this is a distinct possibility, of course, but it has a relatively simple solution.

When a candidate is interested in taking a run at any reasonably high office, he goes around to various places and asks for money.

When you ask someone for a few thousand dollars, naturally, his first question is going to be: "What are you going to do for me in return?"

Early on in any particular political race, there are quite a number of candidates. Anyone who wants to donate money to a political candidate in the hopes of gaining political favors down the road is only going to do so if he believes that the candidate will fulfill the unwritten obligation – the "anti-social contract," if you like.

In politics, as in business, credibility is efficiency. Those who have built up reputations for keeping their promises end up being able to do business on a handshake, which keeps their costs down considerably. No new person entering a field will have the credibility or track record to be able to achieve this enviable efficiency, and so will have to earn it over the course of many years.

Thus we know for certain that when a company gives money to a political candidate, in the expectation of return favors in the future, that political candidate already has an excellent track record of doing just that. This kind of information will have been passed around certain communities – "Joe X is a man of his word!" – just as the reliability of a drug dealer and the quality of his product is passed around in certain other communities.

Thus we know that any candidate who receives significant funding from special interest groups is a man who has consistently proven his "integrity to corruptibility" in the past – for if he has no track record, or an inconsistent track record, no one will give him money to get started.

(Just as a side note, this is a very interesting example of exactly why anarchism will work – we do not need the state to enforce contracts, since the state *itself* functions on implicit contracts that can never be legally enforced.)

In other words, whenever you see a name on the ballot, you can be completely certain that that name represents a man who has already been bought and paid for over the course of many years, and that those who have paid for him do not have, let us say, your best interests at heart.

But we can go one step further.

Since all the money that moves around in a political system must come from somewhere – the millions of dollars that are given to the sugar farmers must come from taxpayers – we can be sure that just about every benefit that special interest groups seek to gain comes at your expense. Pharmaceutical companies want an extension on their patents so they can charge you more money. Domestic steel companies want to increase barriers against imported steel so they can charge you more money. If a government union wants additional benefits, that will cost you. If the police want to expand the war on drugs, that will cost you security, safety and money.

Whoever strives to benefit from the public purse has their hand groping towards *your* pocket.

Thus it is perfectly fair and reasonable to remind you that every name that you see on the ballot is diametrically opposed to your particular and personal interests, since they have been paid for by people who want to rob you blind.

Another aspect of "democricide" is the inevitable and constant escalation of public spending necessary to achieve or maintain political power.

Let us take the example of a mayor running for his second term. When he was running for his first term, sewage treatment workers donated $20,000 to his campaign, and in return he granted them a 10% raise. Now that he is running for his second term, and cannot give them another 10% raise, they have no reason to donate to his campaign. Thus he either has to offer the sewage treatment workers some other benefit, or he has to create some new program or benefit which he can dangle in front of some new group, in order to secure their donations. This is why political candidates always announce new spending when they throw their hats into the ring – the new spending is the rather unsubtle promise of benefits which will be granted to those who donate to his campaign. A new stadium, a new convention center, a new bridge, a new arts program, new housing projects, highway expansions and so on – all of these inevitably and permanently raise the "high water mark" of governmental spending, and are an absolute requirement of running for office.

Now, our aforementioned sewage treatment workers would of course prefer a permanent 10% raise rather than a one-time cash bonus. Thus they will always try to negotiate a permanent contract rather than continue to be at the mercy of the will and whim of their political masters.

As this process continues, the proportion of non-discretionary spending in any political budget grows and grows. This is another reason why new spending initiatives must always be created in order to secure new donations. Money cannot be shifted from one area to another, because it has permanently been earmarked for a particular group in return for a one-time political contribution in the past.

If the mayor who is running for his second term decides to attempt to roll back the 10% raise, in order to free up money which he can then offer to someone else in return for campaign contributions, he would be committing political suicide. He would be breaking a freely-signed contract, sticking it to the working man, and provoking a very smelly strike – but for his own particular self-interest, the effects would be even worse.

Remember, people will donate to a political campaign based on an implicit contract of future rewards from the public treasury. If a candidate attempts to "roll back" benefits that he has distributed previously in return for donations, not only will he incur the wrath of the existing special-interest group, but he will be revealed as a man who breaks his implicit and unenforceable "contracts." Since this candidate can no longer be relied upon to give public money back to those who donate to his campaign, he will find that his campaign donations dry up almost immediately, and his political career comes to an abrupt end.

Of course, ex-politicians are highly prized as lobbyists as well, but if this mayor breaks faith with a donor, he will no longer be valuable in *that* capacity either, and will forego significant income in his post-political career.

Finally, any political candidate who has channeled public money to past donors faces the problem of blackmail. If he attempts to cross any of his prior supporters, mysterious leaks to the press will start to emerge, talking about the sleazy backroom deals that got him in power – thus also effectively ending his political career. All the other candidates will piously deride his cynical corruption, while of course making their own sleazy backroom deals in turn.

(It is highly instructive to note that two well-known fictional portrayals of the political campaign process – "The West Wing" and "The Wire" – repeatedly portray the candidate begging for money, but never *once* show why he receives it – the motives of his donors. The reason for this is simple: they wish to portray an idealistic politician, and so they cannot possibly reveal the reasons why people are giving him money. If the fictional story were to follow the inevitable "laws" of democracy, the storyline would be abruptly truncated, or the lead character would be revealed as far less sympathetic. The candidate would ask for money, and then the potential donor would indicate the favor he wanted in return. Then, the candidate would either refuse, thus ending his campaign for lack of funds – or he would agree, thus ending any real sympathy we have for him. This basic truth – like so many in a statist society – can never be discussed, even on a show like "The Wire," which has little problem revealing corruption everywhere else. A policeman can be shown breaking a child's fingers, but the true nature of the political process must be forever hidden…)

Thus we can see that – at least at the level of economics – democracy is a sort of slow-motion suicide, in which you are told that it is the highest civic virtue to approve of those who want to rob you.

I do not want this book to become a critique of democracy – but rather, as I have said before, my goal is simply to help you to understand the myriad contradictions involved in any logical or moral defense of a state-run society.

If you do not even know that society is sick, you will never be interested in a cure.

THE SOCIAL CHALLENGES OF ANARCHISM

In the interests of efficiency – both yours and mine – I have decided to keep this book as short as possible. If I have not shown you at least some the logical and moral problems with our existing way of organizing society by now, I doubt that I shall ever be able to.

If we accept that perhaps some of the criticisms of statism presented in this little book are at least potentially somewhat valid, one essential question remains.

If you can easily understand the above simple and effective criticisms – compared to, say, the mathematics behind the theory of relativity – then the question must be asked:

"Why have you never heard of these criticisms?"

This question packs more of a punch than you may realize.

If I put forward the charge that our society is currently organized along the principles of violence, control and brutal punishment, but you have never heard this argument before, despite the eager talents of tens of thousands of well-paid intellectuals, professors, pundits, journalists, writers and so on, then there must be some reason – or series of reasons – why such a universal silence remains in place.

The standards of proof for startling new theories must be raised exactly to the degree that those new theories are easy to understand. New theories that are very hard to understand are easier to accept as potentially true, simply because of their difficulty. New theories that are very easy to understand, however, face a far higher hurdle, since they must explain why they have not been understood, discussed or disseminated before.

In this final section, I will talk about why I think anarchism is almost never openly discussed – and is in fact constantly scorned, feared and derided – and I will present what I think is an interesting paradox, which is that *the degree to which anarchism remains undiscussed is exactly the degree to which anarchism will undoubtedly work.*

ANARCHISM AND ACADEMIA

Let's have a look at academia, focusing on the Arts, where anarchism could be a potential topic – areas such as Political Science, Economics, History, Philosophy, Sociology etc.

It is true that a few intellectuals have had successful careers while expressing sympathy for anarchism – on the left, we have the example of Noam Chomsky; in the libertarian camp, we have the example of Murray Rothbard. However, the vast majority of academics simply roll their eyes if and when the subject of anarchism as a viable alternative to a violence-based society ever arises.

To understand this, the first thing that we need to recognize about academia is that, since it is highly subsidized by governments, demand vastly outstrips supply. In other words, there are far more people who want to become academics then there are jobs in academia.

Normally what would occur in this situation – were academia actually part of the free market – is that wages and perks would decline to the point where equilibrium would be reached.

At the moment, academics get several months off during the summer, do not labor under oppressive course loads, are virtually impossible to fire once they reach tenure, get to spend their days reading, writing and discussing ideas (which many of us would consider a hobby), travel with expenses paid to conferences, receive high levels of social respect, get paid sabbatical leaves, a full array of highly lucrative benefits, and can choose comfortable retirements or continued involvement in academia, as they see fit – and often make salaries in the six figures to boot!

Given the number of non-monetary benefits involved in being an academic, in a free market situation, wages would fall precipitously, or job requirements would rise. However, since academics – particularly in the US – basically work under the protection of a highly subsidized union, this does not occur.

Since the job itself is so innately desired by so many people, what results is a "sellers market," in which dozens of qualified candidates jostle for each individual job. Like Angelina Jolie in a nightclub, those with the most to offer can be enormously picky.

Also, since academics cannot be fired, if a department head hires an unpleasant, troublesome, difficult or just unnerving person, he will have to live with that decision for the next 30-odd years. If divorce became impossible, people would be much more careful about choosing compatible spouses.

This is one simple and basic explanation for the exaggerated politeness and conviviality in the world of academia. People who are cantankerous, or who ask uncomfortable questions, or who reason from first principles and thus eliminate endless debating, or whose positions place into question the value and ethics of those around them, simply do not get hired.

In a free market situation, original and challenging thinking would be of great interest to students, who would doubtless pay a premium to be mentally stimulated in such a way. However, since the majority of funding in academia comes from governments, students have virtually no influence over the hiring of professors.

Let us imagine the progress of a wannabe anarchist graduate student.

In his undergraduate classes, he will annoy the professors and irritate his fellow students by asking uncomfortable questions that they cannot answer. If he talks about the violence that is at the root of state funding, he will also be open to the charge of rank hypocrisy – which I can assure you will be lavishly supplied – since he is accepting state money in the form of a subsidized university education.

His implicit criticism of his professors – that they are funded and secured through violence – will be highly annoying to them. Although this anarchist may grind his discontented way through an undergraduate degree, he will find it very hard to get any kinds of letters of reference from his professors to gain entrance into graduate school. If a professor talks about the applicant's anarchism in his letter of recommendation, anyone evaluating such a letter will be utterly bewildered as to why such a recommendation is being made – thus devaluing any such letters from said professor in the future.

If the professor who recommends an anarchist finds that his future recommendations fall on more skeptical eyes, then the word will very quickly spread that taking this professor's course, and getting a letter of recommendation from him, is the kiss of death for any academic aspirant.

Thus this professor will find enrollment in his courses mysteriously declining, which will not be helpful to his career, to say the least.

If the professor does not mention the grad student applicant's anarchism, his fate becomes even worse, since even more time will be wasted interviewing an applicant that no one actually wants. Those on the receiving end of such a letter of recommendation will find it impossible to believe that the professor did not know that the student's anarchism was a factor, and so will view his letter as a bizarre form of passive aggression, and will be that much *less* likely to view any future recommendations even remotely positively.

Thus an academic who writes a letter of recommendation for a student whose views will be disconcerting or discomfiting to others is undermining his value to his future students for no clear benefit whatsoever. We can safely assume that an academic who has reached the rank of professor – even prior to tenure – is not a man blind to his own long-term self-interest.

Even if this anarchist were to somehow get through to a Masters program, the same problems would exist, although they would be even worse than his undergraduate degree. Those who are in a Masters program – particularly in the Arts – are mostly there with the specific goal of securing a position in academia. In other words, they are not there for the relentless pursuit of inviolate truth, but rather to ingratiate themselves with their professors, do the kind of research that will get them noticed, and gain the kind of approval from those above them that will give them a boost up the next rung of the ladder.

Thus, when the anarchist begins talking about his theories, he will face either passive or aggressive hostility from those around him, who will view him as an irritating and counterproductive time-waster. Whether or not his theories are true is actually beside the point – the reality is that his theories actively interfere with the pursuit of academic success, which is why people are in the classroom in the first place.

Also, since the anarchist claims the power to see through the universal veneer of proclaimed self-interest to the core motivations beneath – yet does *not* see the core motivations of those around him in graduate school – he will also be seen to be obstinately blind. "You should believe the truth," he will say, without seeing that these academic aspirants are not there for the truth, but rather to get a job in academia. In other words, *he* is avoiding the truth as much as they are.

Furthermore, by continually reminding people that the existing society in general – and academics in particular – is funded through violence, the anarchist is actively offending and insulting everyone around him. There are very few people who can absorb the moral charge of blindness to evil and corruption and come back with open-mindedness and curiosity.

If the anarchist is right, then the professors are corrupt, and the academic aspirants should really abandon their fields and go into the private sector, or become self-employed, or something along those lines. However, these people have already invested years of their lives and hundreds of thousands of dollars in lost income in pursuit of a position in academia. They obviously do not want a position in the free market, since they are in a graduate arts degree program – and should they leave that program, a good portion of the entire value that they have accumulated will vanish.

We could examine this process for much longer, but let us end with this point.

Let us imagine that a tenured academic reads this book and agrees with at least the potential validity of some of the arguments it contains. He does not have to really worry about getting fired, so why would he not begin to raise these questions with his colleagues?

Well, because these views will discredit him with his colleagues, display what they would consider "poor judgment," (and in some ways they would not be wrong!) and this would have a highly deleterious effect on his ability to get published, speak at conferences, attract students, and enjoy a convivial and collegial work environment with his peers.

He will thus harm his own pleasure, career and interests, without changing anyone's mind about anarchism – so why would he pursue such a course?

When an environment is corrupt, rational self-interest is automatically and irredeemably corrupted as well. We can see this easily in the realm of politics, but it is harder to see in the realm of academia.

Before I started this section, I said that I would present an interesting paradox, which is that *the degree to which anarchism remains undiscussed is exactly the degree to which anarchism will undoubtedly work*.

Anarchism is fundamentally predicated on the basic reality that violence is *not required* to organize society. Violence in the form of self-defense is acceptable, of course, but the *initiation* of the use of force is not only morally evil, but counterproductive from a pragmatic standpoint as well.

Anarchism – at least as I approach it – is not a form of relentless pacifism which rejects any coercive responses to violence. My formulation of an anarchistic society is one which has perfectly powerful and capable mechanisms for dealing with violent crime, in the absence of a centralized group of criminals called the state. In fact, an anarchistic society will undoubtedly deal with the problems of violent crime in a far more proactive and beneficial manner than our existing systems, which in fact do far more to provoke violence and criminality than they do to reduce or oppose it.

Anarchists recognize the power of implicit and voluntary social contract, and the power of both positive incentives such as pay and career success, as well as negative incentives such as social disapproval, economic exclusion and outright ostracism.

Thus in a very interesting way, the more that anarchism is *excluded* from the social discourse, the greater belief anarchists can have in the practicality of their own solutions.

In the realm of academia, obviously there is no central coercive committee that will shoot or imprison anyone who brings up anarchism in a positive light – there is no "state" in the realm of the university, yet the "rules" are universally respected and enforced, spontaneously, without planning, without coordination – and without violence!

This irony becomes even greater in the realm of politics, where the implicit "contracts" of political backroom deals are universally enforced through a process of positive selection for corruption, in that those who do not "pay back" their contributors with public money are automatically excluded from the system.

Thus both academia and the state itself work on anarchistic principles, which is the spontaneous self-organization and enforcement of unwritten rules without relying on violence.

A truly stateless society, where such rules could be made explicit and openly contractual, would function even *more* effectively.

In other words, if anarchism were openly talked about in state-funded academia, it would be very likely that anarchism would never work in practice.

If the unenforceable corruption of democracy did not "work" so well, that would be a significant blow against the practical efficacy of anarchism.

ACADEMICS AND VOLUNTARISM

Academics face an enormous challenge – particularly in economics – which is the charge of rank hypocrisy.

Economists are nearly universal in their support for free trade, yet of course most economists work in state-funded or state-supported institutions such as universities, the World Bank, the IMF and so on – and in academia in particular, take shelter behind enormously high barriers to entry in the form of institutionalized protectionism, and shield themselves from market forces through tenure.

Economists have a number of sophisticated responses to the question why, if voluntarism and free markets are so good, do they specifically exclude *themselves* from the push and pull of the free market?

First of all, academics will argue, the truth of a proposition is not determined by the integrity of the proposer (if Hitler says that two plus two is four, we cannot reasonably oppose him by saying that he is evil). Secondly, many academics will say that they have merely *inherited* the system from prior academics, and that they held these free-market views before they achieved tenure. Thirdly, they can argue that they do face possible unemployment, however unlikely, should their department close, and so on.

These are all very interesting arguments, and are worthy of our attention I think, but are fundamentally irrelevant to the question of academia.

It is a common defense of hypocritical intellectuals to say that their arguments cannot be judged by their own contradictory behaviour, but must be viewed on their own merits – but this argument *does* become rather tiresome after a while.

To see what I mean, let us imagine a man named Bob who claims that his sole professional goal in life is motivating others to lose weight by following his diet. He continually proclaims that it is very important to be slim, and that only *his* diet will make you slim – but strangely enough, Bob himself remains morbidly obese!

It is certainly true that we cannot absolutely judge the efficacy and value of Bob's diet solely by how much he weighs – but we can empirically judge whether or not *Bob* believes in the efficacy and value of his own diet.

Life is short, and the more rapidly we can make accurate decisions, the better off we are.

Imagine that, this afternoon, a disheveled and smelly man stops you on the street and offers his services as a financial advisor, but says that he cannot take your phone calls because after he declared personal bankruptcy, he has been forced to live in his car. It is certainly logically true that we cannot empirically use his situation to judge the value of his financial advice – but we can know for sure the following: *either he has followed his own financial advice, which has clearly resulted in a disaster, or he has not, which means that he does not believe that it is either valuable or true.*

Thus, based on the principles of mere efficiency, you would *never* hire such a vagrant as your trusted financial adviser – partly also due to the basic fact that he seems completely oblivious to the effect that his approach has on his credibility. Does he not recognize how you will view him, based on his presentation? If he does not realize how he appears to you, this also indicates his near-complete disconnect from reality.

In the same way, if I show up for a job interview wearing only a pair of underpants, two clothes-pins and a colander, it is clearly true that my choice of dress cannot be objectively used to judge the quality of my professional knowledge – but it certainly is the case that my judgment *as a whole* can be somewhat called into question, to say the least.

If you do not follow your own advice, I cannot *ipso facto* use that to judge your advice as incorrect, but I certainly *can* judge that *you* believe your advice to be incorrect, and make a completely rational decision about its value thereby.

Academics claim that their teachings are designed to have some effect in the outside world. No medical school teaches Klingon anatomy, because such "knowledge" would have no effect in the world.

Economists teach ideas so that better solutions can be implemented in the real world, which we know because they constantly complain that governments ignore their economic advice. In other words, they are frustrated because politicians constantly choose personal career goals over objectively valuable actions and decisions.

If I am trying to sell a diet book, and I am morbidly obese, obviously that totally undermines my credibility. What is the best way, then, for me to increase my credibility? Is it for me to endlessly complain that other people just don't seem to believe in my diet?

Of course not.

The simple solution is for me to apply my efforts to that which I actually have control over – my own eating – *and stop nagging other people to do what I obviously do not want to do.*

This way, I can actually gain even *more* credibility than I would have had if I had been naturally slim to begin with. Since most people who want to diet are overweight, surely a man who loses a lot of weight – and keeps it off – by following his own diet has even *more* credibility!

What does this translate to in the realm of academics?

Well, almost all economists accept that free trade is the best way to organize economic interactions – thus they have the enormous collective advantage of already sharing common ideals, which is scarcely the case with politicians and other groups that economists criticize for failing to implement free trade.

If economists believe that free market voluntarism is the best way to organize interactions – and clearly they have far more control over their *own* profession than they do over governments – then they should work as hard as they can *to apply those principles to their own profession.* To lose their *own* excess weight, so to speak, rather than endlessly nag other people to follow the diet that they themselves reject.

Thus rather than lecture about the virtues and values of a voluntary free-market – with the clear goal of changing the behavior of others – economists should get together and change their *own* profession to reflect the values that they expect others to follow.

This way, they can do all the research, keep careful notes and publish papers describing the process of getting an organization to reform itself according to the commonly-accepted values of its members. The pitfalls and challenges of achieving such a noble end would be well worth documenting, as a guide and help to others.

Furthermore, since economists all believe that free trade improves quality and productivity, they could as a group measure the quality and productivity of the economics profession before and after the introduction of free trade and voluntarism. This would be an enormously valuable body of research, and would empirically support the case for going through the challenges of undoing protectionism within a profession.

Since academics very much want to have an effect on the outside world, by far the best way of achieving that goal is to reform their own profession to reflect the values that they already profess and hold as a group. They can then bring their own experience – not to mention integrity – to bear on the far greater challenges of helping governments and other organizations reform themselves.

It is quite fascinating that economists – to my limited knowledge at least – have produced virtually endless studies on the negative effects of protectionism *in every conceivable field except their own.*

If economists *do* take on the challenge of reforming their own profession according to their own commonly-held values, either such a revolution will succeed, or it will not.

If the revolution succeeds, academics would have the theoretical understanding, empirical evidence and professional credibility to bring their case for free trade to others, with a far greater chance of being successful.

If the revolution does not succeed, then clearly economists would have to give up the pretense that their arguments could ever have any effect on the outside world, and could begin the process of dismantling their own profession, since it would be revealed as little more than a fraud – the "selling" of a diet that was impossible to follow.

If economists cannot achieve conformity to their values within their own profession, where they share very similar methodologies, have the same goals, and speak the same language, then clearly asking other professions – with far greater obstacles – to reform themselves is ridiculously hypocritical, and fundamentally false.

I am sure that economists have far too much personal and professional integrity to take money for "snake oil" solutions that can never be implemented.

Thus I eagerly look forward to these economists taking their own advice, and reforming their own profession, where they have *real* control, in order to show other people that it can be done – and how it should be done – and to, as a group, truly achieve the goals that they so nobly profess as their main motivation.

What do you think the odds of this occurring are?

This is why you have never heard of anarchism.

ANARCHY AND SOCIALIZING

Human beings are so constituted – and I in no way think that this is a bad thing of course – to be exquisitely good at negotiating cost/benefit scenarios. This ability is fundamental to all forms of organic life, in that those who are unsuccessful at calculating these scenarios are quickly weeded out of the gene pool – but human beings possess this ability at a staggeringly brilliant conceptual level.

If you have gotten this far in this book, I can tell at least a few things about you. Obviously, you are curious and open-minded, and largely un-offended by original arguments, as long as they at least strive for rationality. I strongly doubt that you are in academia – or if you are, I fully expect lengthy, obtuse and condescending attacks on my arguments to appear in my inbox, or on your blog, within a few hours.

Potential academics have in my experience been irredeemably hostile to what I do because it puts them in an exquisitely tortuous position (this is particularly the case with my book "Universally Preferable Behavior: A Rational Proof of Secular Ethics").

Wannabe academics have to believe that they are motivated by the pursuit of truth, not of tenure. Given that they have to ingratiate themselves with their academic masters, they must also believe that their professors are motivated by the pursuit of truth as well, not of power, salary and tenure. We can honorably submit ourselves to a moral teacher; we cannot honorably submit ourselves to an amoral teacher.

If academics is about the pursuit of truth, then my particular contributions to the field should at least garner some interest, if only because of the success I have had with laypeople. However, a wannabe grad student will face extreme anxiety at even the *thought* of bringing some of my work to the attention of his professors, because he knows what their reaction will be – scorn, dismissal, cynical laughter or genial bewilderment – and also that by bringing my work to his professors, he will be undermining the forward progress of his academic career.

Thus what I do is tortuous, particularly to graduate students, because it reveals to them the basic reality of academia, which is that it is not largely to do with the pursuit of truth, but rather is about the currying of influence and favor, and the pursuit of career goals – inevitably, at the expense of the truth itself.

When this is revealed, the long barren stretch of half a decade or more required to pursue and achieve a Ph.D. becomes a desert that truly feels too broad to cross. The anxiety and despair that my work evokes creates fear and hostility – and it is far easier to take that out on me then to question or criticize the academic system or the professors whose approval these moral heroes depend upon.

Furthermore, questioning the moral roots of the system they are embedded in will simply get them ejected from that system (just as anarchistic theory would predict) and will in no way reform that system, or change anyone's mind within it, or improve the quality of teaching. Thus those who remain will inevitably tell themselves the comforting lie that the system is flawed, granted, but that leaving it would be to abandon one's post, so to speak, and so the practical and moral thing to do is to struggle through, and improve the quality of teaching as best one can in the future.

Of course, this is all utterly impossible, but it is a tantalizing mythology that does help the average grad student sleep at night.

The reason that I'm talking about these kinds of calculations is that we all face this choice in life when we are presented with a startling and unforeseen argument that we cannot dismantle. Our truly brilliant ability to process cost/benefit scenarios immediately kicks out a series of syllogisms such as the following:

- Anarchist arguments are valid BUT…
- I will never have any influence on the elimination of the state in my lifetime;
- I will alienate, frustrate and bewilder those around me by bringing these arguments up;
- I will not have any influence on the thinking of those around me;
- If people have to choose between the truth that I bring and their own illusions, they will ditch both me and the truth without as much as a backward glance.
- Thus I will have alienated myself from those around me, for the sake of a goal I can never achieve.

These sorts of calculations flash rapidly through our minds, resulting in an irritation towards the arguments that can never be directly expressed, and fear of any further examination of the truth of one's social and professional relations.

Society is really an ecosystem of agreed-upon premises or arguments, usually based on tradition. Those who accept the "truth" of these arguments find their practical course through the existing social infrastructure enormously eased; they do not ask people to really *think*, they do not discomfort others with uncomfortable truths, and thus what passes for discourse in the world resembles more two mirrors facing each other – a narrow infinity of empty reflection, if you will pardon the metaphor.

When a new idea attempts to enter into the intellectual bloodstream of society, so to speak, those who have placed their bets on the continuance of the existing belief structure react as any biological defense system would, with a combination of *attack* and *isolation*.

When you get an infection, your immune system will first attempt to kill off the bacteria; if it is unable to do that, it will attempt to isolate it, forming a hard shell or cyst around the infection.

In a similar way, when a new idea "infects" the existing ecosystem of social thinking, intellectuals will first attempt to ignore it, but then will attempt to "kill it off" using a wide variety of emotionally manipulative tricks, such as scorn, eye-rolling, cynical laughter, aggression, insults, condescension, *ad hominem* attacks and so on.

If these aggressive tactics do not work for some reason, then the fallback position is a rigid attempt to "isolate" those who support the new paradigm.

These tactics are so staggeringly effective that hundreds or thousands of years can pass between significant new intellectual movements and achievements. The last great leaps forward in Western thinking, it could be argued, occurred around the time of the Enlightenment, several hundred years ago, when the new ideas of the free market, and the power and validity of the scientific method emerged. ("Democracy" and the "separation of church and state" were not new concepts, but were inherited from the expanding interest in Roman jurisprudence that occurred after the 14th century through the rise of cities, and the subsequent necessity for more comprehensive and detailed civic laws.) Since then, there have been some dramatic increases in personal liberties – notably, the non-enforcement of slavery and the expansion of property rights for women, but in the 20th century, most of the "new" developments in human thinking tended to be tribal throwbacks, irrational in theory and evil in practice, such as fascism, communism, socialism, collectivism and so on.

Society "survives" by accepting a fairly rigid set of unquestionable axioms. If people start poking around at the root of those axioms, they are first ignored, then attacked, then isolated. Individuals have almost no ability to overturn these core axioms within their own lifetimes – and thus it takes a somewhat "irrational" dedication to truth and reason to take this course.

This is also something that I know about you…

Socrates described himself as a "gadfly" that buzzed around annoying those in society through his persistent questioning – but he himself was bothered by an internal "gadfly" which constantly nagged at him with these same problems.

Given the extraordinarily high degree of discomfort that is generated by questioning social axioms, I know for sure that you are also possessed by one of these internal "Socratic daemons" which will not let you rest in the face of irrationality, or remain content with pseudo-answers to essential questions.

Now that I have opened up at least the possibility of these answers up in your mind, I know that you will keep returning to them, almost involuntarily, turning them over, looking for weaknesses – because of a kind of obsession that you have, or a mania for consistency with reason and evidence.

There are very few of us who, in some sort of Rawlsian scenario, would get on bended knee before birth and demand to be granted this kind of obsessive compulsive dedication to philosophical truth. Given the high degree of social inconvenience, the resulting anxiety, hostility and isolation, and the near-certainty that we shall not live to see the truth we know accepted at large, it would seem to be almost a form of masochism to reopen arguments which everyone else accepts as both proven and moral. We might as well be a police detective questioning a case with 200 eyewitnesses, a confession, and a smoking gun. Just as this detective would be viewed as annoying, irrational and strange...

Well, I'm sure that you get the picture, because you *live* in this picture.

Thus in attempting to answer the question as to why these ideas, though rational and relatively simple to understand, remain unspoken and unexamined, we can see that any purely *practical* calculation of the costs and benefits of bringing these issues up, either in academics, or in one's own personal social circle, would lead any reasonable person to avoid these thoughts for the same reason that we would give a hissing cobra a wide berth.

Of course, the reason that society does progress at all is because all thinking men and women pay at least a surface lip-service to the principles of reason and evidence.

The corruption and falsification of social discourse that inevitably results from state-funded intellectualism represents an enormously powerful and seemingly-overwhelming "front" that can forever keep a rational examination of core premises at bay.

Unfortunately for the academics – though fortunately for us – the rise of the Internet has to at least some degree diminished the threat of isolation, so that those of us dedicated to "truth at all costs" can never be fully isolated from social interaction, even if we must be satisfied with the arm's-length intimacy of digital relationships.

Whereas in the past I would have had to endure a crippling and futile isolation from those around me, which would have very likely broken my spirit and my desire for "truth at all costs," I can now converse freely with like-minded people at any time, day or night.

The cost of "the truth at all costs" has thus come down considerably, making it a far more attractive pursuit.

Anarchism and Integrity

Without a doubt, there is no conceivable way to make the case that you should examine or explore anarchy in order to achieve anarchistic goals at a political level. That would be like asking Francis Bacon, the founder of the modern scientific method, to pursue his ideas in order to secure funding for a particle accelerator.

When I was younger, I studied acting and playwriting for two years at the National Theater School in Montréal, Canada. On our very first day, we eager thespians were told that if we could be happy doing anything other than acting, we should do that other thing. Acting is such an irrational career to pursue that no sane calculation of the costs and benefits would ever lead anyone in that direction.

In the same way, if you can be happy and content without examining the core assumptions held by those around you, I would strongly suggest that you never bring the contents of this book up with anyone, and look at what is written about here as a mere unorthodox intellectual exercise, like examining the gameplay that might result from alternate chess rules.

If it is the case, however, that you have a passion for the truth – or, as it more often feels, that the truth has an unwavering passion for *you* – then the discontentedness and alienation that you have always felt can be profitably alleviated through an exploration of philosophical truth.

Once we begin to cross-examine our own core beliefs – the prejudices that we have inherited from history – we will inevitably face the feigned indifference, open hostility and condescending scorn from those around us, particularly those who claim to have an expertise in the matters we explore.

This can all be painful and bewildering, it is true – on the other hand, however, once we develop a truly deep and intimate relationship with the truth – and thus, really, with our own selves – we will find ourselves almost involuntarily looking back upon our own prior relationships and truly seeing for the first time the shallowness and evasion that characterized our interactions. We can never be closer to others than we are to ourselves, and we can never be closer to ourselves than we are to the truth – the truth leads us to personal authenticity; authenticity leads us to intimacy, which is the greatest joy in human relations.

Thus while it is true that while many shallow people will pass from our lives when we pursue the "truth at all costs," it is equally true that across the desert of isolation lies a small village – it is not yet a city, nor even a town – full of honest and passionate souls, where love and friendship can flower free of hypocrisy, selfishness and avoidance, where curious and joyful self-expression flow easily, where the joy of honesty and the fundamental relaxation of easy self-criticism unifies our happy tribe in our pursuit and achievement of the truth.

The road to this village is dry, and long, and stony, and hard.

I truly hope that you will join us.

Printed in Great Britain
by Amazon